# The Enlightened Machine

# The Enlightened Machine

## An Analytical Introduction to Neuropsychology

**Daniel N. Robinson**

Columbia University Press    New York    1980

**Library of Congress Cataloging in Publication Data**

Robinson, Daniel N      1937-
The enlightened machine.

Includes bibliographical references and index.
1. Neuropsychology. I. Title. [DNLM: 1. Psycho-
physiology. WL103 R659e]
QP360.R6 1980      612'.8'01      79-29756
ISBN 0-231-04954-4
ISBN 0-231-04955-2 pbk.

Columbia University Press
New York      Guildford, Surrey

Columbia University Press Morningside Edition 1980

Preface to the Morningside Edition
Copyright © Columbia University Press   1980

Printed in the United States of America

To Joseph M. Notterman

# Contents

# Foreword

No mind?
No matter.
No matter?
Never mind.

MacDougal was fond of stating the mind-body problem with these boundary conditions. The most fundamental problem in the history of philosophy and psychology is the relation between our own subjective experience and the external world. For a number of years it had been fashionable in psychology to ignore the problem. However, it refused to go away. There is currently a great resurgence of interest in this most basic of all issues. The work of Roger Sperry on split-brain man and Karl Pribram's brilliant treatise on the "Languages of the Brain" come immediately to mind (they matter!).

Dr. Daniel Robinson makes an important contribution to psychology in this text. *The Enlightened Machine* is an introduction to physiological psychology that confronts the mind-body issue directly and with insight. The book is historically sensitive, yet lively and very modern. Dr. Robinson surveys current and significant issues in physiological psychology from a perspective of their intellectual roots in history and their current significance.

The student will find Dr. Robinson's book a most enjoyable experience—a property shared by all-too-few texts. The instructor will find it satisfactory in terms of necessary coverage of material and very useful as a source of lively controversies. Readers will find *The Enlightened Machine* both enlightening and stimulating.

Richard F. Thompson, Ph.D.
Professor, Department of Psychobiology
University of California (Irvine)

# Preface to the Morningside Edition

*The Enlightened Machine* was written in 1971 and was published in 1973 by Dickenson, which no longer exists. Yet, even under the stresses of corporate failure and dissolution, this little essay went through three printings and was translated into Spanish (*La Maquina Consciente*) as recently as 1977. Critical reviews, both formal and informal, were especially gratifying and, thus, the prospect of the book going out of print was especially disappointing. The Wadsworth Publishing Company, Dickenson's parent, was most cooperative in returning all copyrights to me soon after Dickenson was "reabsorbed," but I was not particularly hopeful at the time that a new publisher would be interested in reissuing what was already a six-year-old text that had never been intended to capture a large readership.

Early in January 1979, I had the opportunity to give an invited lecture at the annual A.A.A.S. Convention held in Houston, Texas. Professors Barbara Ross and Gregory Kimble had organized a symposium honoring the first century of the Leipzig achievement and had asked a half-dozen scholars to prepare articles for this centennial retrospective. As part of his introduction of me, Professor Kimble made several generous statements about *The Enlightened Machine* and encouraged all attending the session to make a point of reading it. I thanked him for these kind remarks, but was then obliged to inform the audience that the book was no longer in print. *Sic transit gloria libri!*

Alas, the day was not lost. Also present at the symposium was Dr. Vicki Raeburn of Columbia University Press, for whom I had already written *Systems of Modern Psychology: A Critical Sketch.* Dr. Raeburn was sufficiently moved by the praise heaped on *The Enlightened Machine* to ask that a copy be sent to her. Some weeks later, after receiving and reading it, she decided it should be reissued by

Columbia, a decision supported by her referees. In my household, the book has been given the sobriquet, "Lazarus."

I should say a few words about the aims of *The Enlightened Machine* and note the negligible alterations contained in this new edition. First, the book is not now and never was intended as a *textbook* for full courses in Physiological Psychology. One cannot cover in under two-hundred pages what standard texts labor to embrace in five-hundred or even a thousand pages. Rather than a text, then, the book is best considered as an essay; a critical exposition of the principal methods, findings, and perspectives that dominate "neuropsychology" and give it its unique character as a discipline. Throughout, attention is paid to the conceptual dimensions of theory and experiment, and to the vast distance separating research *findings* and bona fide scientific *explanations*. This is the import of the adjective "analytical" in the subtitle. My aim is to introduce the reader not to an exhaustive list of experimental discoveries, but to a representative collection of such discoveries for the purpose of illustrating the nagging problems that attach to all such findings.

The second aim of the book, and one firmly anchored to the first, is to alert the reader to the essentially psychological character of physiological psychology, lest anyone be persuaded that all psychological issues will evaporate once the methods and instruments of the biological sciences have been perfected. In recent years, this hybrid-discipline has entered a new phase of that "identity-crisis" that is so common to all branches of social science. Increasingly, the crisis is temporarily averted by equating physiological psychology with neurophysiology. Indeed, one would be hard-pressed, in reviewing the past decade of research conducted by physiological psychologists, to distinguish their studies from those routinely reported in journals devoted to neurophysiology, neurochemistry, and experimental neurosurgery. What we have here is not an encouraging sign of the impending "unity of the sciences," but a portentous sign that many psychologists have forfeited the traditional and vexing issues of their profession in favor of the safer and more mechanical features of behavior and sensation. But the problems that virtually define psychology will not surrender to indifference. They will persist until they are again confronted head-on by those prepared to accept them on their own terms. I speak here, of course, about the problems of free will, volition, consciousness, language, and thought. Any system of psychology—physiological or otherwise—officially indifferent to these issues is not likely to be taken seriously for long, nor should it be.

Since these objectives would appear to be appropriately considered in any context in which the biological correlates of psychological processes are studied, *The Enlightened Machine* might serve as a useful supplement to texts in a number of courses: Introductory, Experimental, and Physiological Psychology; Introductory Philosophy and Philosophy of Mind; Behavioral Biology, "Sociobiology," and Ethology.

The changes introduced in this new addition are nearly entirely confined to the Notes at the end of each chapter, although a few corrections in the text have also been made. The decision both I and the Press had to make finally was narrowed to a choice between a reprinting and a revised edition, and both the Press and I strongly preferred the former. The justification here, however, was certainly not the belief that the first edition could not be improved, but that a modest book on a vast subject does not lend itself to meaningful revisions. The book's focus is perspectival, not factual or methodological. Accordingly, such findings and techniques as have appeared in physiological psychology since 1971 do not, in and of themselves, constitute a challenge to any of the major principles or arguments contained herein.

Daniel N. Robinson
Georgetown 1980

# 1
# *The Birth of a Science*

Few scientific areas have captured the popular imagination more or seem to relate more cogently to human concerns than the neural sciences. As if the intrinsic glamor of the field were not enough, the full arsenal of modern press-agentry has accompanied recent advances. As a result, the layman is often left believing that "they" are at the threshold of discoveries that may irreversibly alter the destiny of his species. With the media striking that unhappy balance of just too little information and just too much exaggeration, he sees posterity caught in the clutches of "genetic engineers," "bio-feedback technologists," mind-manipulating neurochemists.

Such fears are irrational but understandable. I will not attempt here to reduce them or to intensify them. Instead, we will briefly explore the origins of the neural sciences, their philosophical foundations, their principal methods and findings, and the logical basis upon which they rest their hypotheses. Much of the emphasis must be on definitions. If one fears that another is longing or able to control his "mind," he must have some ideas of what the word *mind* means. And if it's the neural scientist he is worried about—that specialist who studies the nervous system—then he must have concluded that, whatever "mind" is, it is determined by the brain. If these two words, *mind* and *brain,* seem to be synonymous, the balance of the book should give some pause.

The principal objective of this book, then, is to introduce the discipline of neuropsychology. A discipline is a collection of problems, methods, perspectives, and basic assumptions. Neuropsychology makes use of chemistry, physiology, anatomy, physics, mathematics. But it is not these fields, nor is it some combination of them. Thus, the text treats topics drawn from other sciences only to the extent that they relate to the subject matter of neuropsychology; that is, the relationship between neural events and psychological functions. There will be no interest in nerves for the sake of nerves or molecules for the sake of molecules. However, should a molecule offer itself as a *memory*, it will be scrutinized with overweaning interest. The tone of the book is critical (in the analytical sense) and not simply descriptive. A collection of facts is no more an argument than a collection of bricks is a house. What I hope to achieve is an appreciation for the *meaning* of the facts, and this appreciation depends more upon their nature than their number.

## ORIGINS

Science is the perpetual childhood of philosophy. When we observe a child with a new toy, we can learn something about man's methods of scientific discovery. He picks it up, twists and tastes it, feels it everywhere, and, in one way or another, attempts to ascertain its function. Does it roll? Will it bounce? Can it break? The last question is the most fundamental. As he removes its ears or pulls off its wheels, he is discovering what it is, what it is made of, what it *reduces* to. He learns that, in its entirety, it is "horsee" and that its parts are "ears," "nose," "tail." With added experience and instruction, he learns that while "horsee" and "bow-wow" are not the same, ears and tails and noses are. They occupy the same relative positions, have similar shapes, serve analogous functions. Shown the ears and noses and tails of toy horses and toy dogs, the child soon knows which animal owns what, but he never thinks that the ear *is* a horse or that the nose *is* a dog. Rather, they are attributes or what more technically may be called reliable correlates of these animals. So even the primitive intelligence of the child can distinguish between things and their attributes. But now the task becomes more difficult. We give a formless object the eyes, ears, nose, mouth, etc., of a horse. The child immediately calls it "horse" and, in so doing, reveals his conception of essence. The essence of *horse* is the sum of its parts. (See Figure 1-1.)

At this point, we are not simply dealing with childish concepts. We are also confronting a philosophical question of the first order. For what if we place a dog's ears on the model of a horse? Are they now, by that fact, horse's ears? Or is the horse now a dog? And what are ears? Are they organs of hearing? But then the spider's legs are ears, and now what are legs? No child and very few adults are interested in

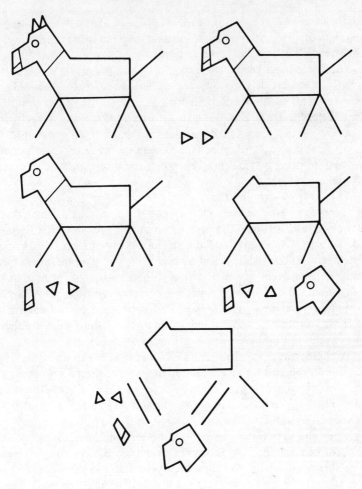

**FIGURE 1-1**
When is it no longer "Bow-wow"?

such questions, but without them an understanding of the modern neural sciences is not mature.

Questions of this kind began in ancient Greece, when man and the world were first seen as exciting new toys to be touched, turned upside down, and reduced to their elements. Only a shallow sampling of those impishly titanic minds—Democritus, Socrates, Plato, Aristotle—is warranted here. We borrow just a small fraction of their genius to help illuminate the subject of our present concern, the mind. To set the stage for this review, we must realize that the same words can mean different things when used in different times. In the pre-

Socratic era of the Homeric poets, *psyche* (from which the word *psychology* is formed) meant *soul*, as it does in Greek to this day. But the meaning of *soul* in Homeric times was different from its meaning in Socratic times. To the Homerics, *soul* was the mystical spirit of the deep—an ethereal, vaporous entity that would leave the body and wander through the world collecting the substance of our dreams. It was different from the life-giving force (*spirtu*) and largely independent of the forces of consciousness and reason (*pneuma*).[1]* In fact, this latter word was incorporated into seventeenth-century writing on psychological matters when the discipline was referred to as *pneumatology*.

The Greeks invented these words to represent the unseen causes of everyday experience. They wanted to explain dreams, fits, madness, intoxication—the myriad circumstances in which the mind takes leave of the body, and the senses betray our wits. In Homeric times, ignorance was disguised by recourse to mysterious agents, by a faith in omnipotent energies with a will and a design for human life. The principal expository vehicle was poetry, and the most popular explanatory device was metaphor. Philosophy had yet to be born, and man was forced to understand through the visions of his teachers rather than through their demonstrations or their logic.

With Socrates, we witness the first example in the entire history of recorded thought of prolonged, patient, and reasoned argument as a method of arriving at "eternal" truths. The older Orient, the Egyptians, the civilizations of Minos and Mycenae—all had highly developed systems of thought. They could boast of advanced technologies and agricultural sciences. But none had philosophy. Pharaoh told the masses the law but never examined the meaning of justice. Siddhartha Gautama, the Buddha, urged India to join in ascetic simplicity that it may know the good life. But what is the end? What is good? What is true? No argument is offered. And even if the teachings could somehow be established as *facts*, they are not *reasoned facts*. With Socrates the format changed. The opposition is given a voice, and the arguments are forced to oblige an adversary. "I give you one philosophy after another," Socrates says to Theatetus in the *Phaedo*, "in order that you may come to know your own mind." Here is a statement of the objective: not the happy life, not immortality, not riches, not popular regard, not practical success, but to know one's own mind.

In his psychology, Socrates subscribed to a theory of tensions—tensions between the rational and the sensual, between passion and

*Notes appear at the end of each chapter.

intellect. This view was borrowed no doubt from the austere puritanism of the followers of Pythagoras, who believed that the pleasures of the body infect the purity of the soul. H. L. Mencken once defined puritanism as "the haunting feeling that someone somewhere may be happy." But although the Pythagoreans can be accused of this commitment to joylessness, Socrates had no such austere motives. The Pythagorean mission to free the soul of material encumbrances was an end in itself; furthermore, the Pythagorean soul was a Homeric organ. In contrast, Socrates advocated purification of the soul as the necessary means to a higher end, to *understanding*. In describing the soul as that which can bring understanding, he brought *psyche* out of metaphysical darkness and into the light of nature. He gave it a living purpose and made it an instrument that could be used by man—not, as in earlier times, the force that used man.

Socrates explicitly rejected the senses as means of acquiring understanding. In the Platonic dialogues, we find example after example of the weaknesses of the senses, the limitations of experience, the unreality of the sensible. The eternal verities—the fundamental truths upon which all else is based—are abstractions. They can be known but never sensed. As long as man depends upon his senses, he will be so saturated with the ever changing appearances of things that he will remain blind to the changeless truths of the universe. One may witness a just act, but justice itself makes no appeal to the senses. It can be grasped only through reason, through what is now called *cognition*.

In Socratic and Platonic philosophy, the eternal realities are *ideas* and, over the centuries, such notions have been subsumed under the rubric *idealism*. An idea is more than, and may be very different from, the consequences of sensory activity. That is, an idea is not the same as a perception. One may observe apples fall endlessly without ever having the idea of a gravitational force. One may examine an infinity of right-angle triangles without ever discovering the Pythagorean theorem. An idea is an invention of the mind. It is what the mind does *to* experience rather than what it does *with* experience. When the philosophers asked, "Are Socrates standing and Socrates seated the same Socrates?" they were exploring the *idea* of Socrates.

What are those necessary and sufficient properties of a thing that make it what it is and not something else? We shall raise this question again in connection with the mind and the role of the brain in our idea of the mind. The question about how many Socrates there are is central to the question of experience. As a visual stimulus, Socrates is different every time he or his audience moves. He changes with age, with clothes, with the time of day. But there is some fundamental thing about him that does not change. There is an essence, a real Socrates, not revealed by his changing attributes. So too with truth and with justice and with beauty. A beautiful object may become ugly, but beauty itself is immutable. The senses receive only attributes; the mind locates the essence. To do this, it must contain an intrinsic property that functions apart from and even in defiance of the senses. This intrinsic property is itself the essence of the mind. It is not acquired with experience; it does not change with the seasons. With this view, Socrates and Plato added to *idealism* (a belief in ideas as eternal realities) the philosophic assertion of *nativism*, a belief in the presence of innate ideas.

These were the intellectual traditions into which Aristotle was born and by which he was nurtured. But tradition is only part of a man. The rest is what he makes of it. In many important respects, Aristotle agreed with his mentors; as a practical thinker, however, he saw no necessity to deny the reality of the senses. He argued that most of man's knowledge is gained through the senses; that is, from experience. But knowledge exists in different forms. There is, for example, practical knowledge, the knowledge that guides us in most of our daily life, the knowledge from experience that $X$ is usually followed by $Y$. It gets us in out of the rain. It lets us build a house and light a fire. It is a knowledge based upon facts; it is, in other words, "common sense." There is also a second and rarer kind of knowledge, a form of wisdom. It is a knowledge based upon *reasoned* facts, not merely observations. It is a knowledge of causes, not simply correlations. Where practical knowledge gives us such observations as "$Y$ follows $X$," this more advanced form of knowledge gives us laws. It is a knowledge of necessities; it is *scientific* knowledge. Aristotle, like Plato and Socrates, reasoned that this form of knowledge cannot be gained through perception. The senses detect only what is changeable, while scientific principles are constant. Thus, the senses must feed some sort of intellectual process that takes the bare bits of experience and from them constructs causal explanations.

Notwithstanding his modified idealism, Aristotle emphasized the role of experience and perception to an unprecedented extent. We call him the father of *empiricism* because of this emphasis. He did not assume that sensual and rational processes must compete in heedless conflict. Instead, he assumed that the processes interact. The soul, according to Aristotle, consists of a number of faculties: a perceptive faculty, by which stimuli in the environment gain access to the mind; a rational faculty, by which these perceptions are evaluated and organized into lawful dependencies; a locomotor faculty, by which animals respond to the demands of life. The perceptive and the rational faculties, present together only in man, contribute to and depend upon each other.

Aristotle never did resolve the question of innate ideas, nor has anyone since. The problem is this: If there is nothing within us at the start, how can our experiences ever come to have meaning? How is a certain color perceived as blue, a wound as painful? On the other hand, if there *are* ideas of such things within us at birth, why does the untaught child know so little? Aristotle's answer to these questions is a compromise. No, the ideas themselves are not present at birth, but a certain *capacity* is. Thus, a man and a cow may sense the same sky; because of their different capacities, however, they never "know" the same sky. This is pretty much how the matter has stood for 2,300 years.

At about the same time that idealism and empiricism were competing for philosophical priority, a third and very different perspective existed—the *materialistic* philosophy of Democritus, a brilliant, impatient, and skeptical scholar.

Philosophers seem to be of two distinct species; those who claim that something is more than we think it is and those who assert that it is less. A third variety, far rarer, is found between these two. Democritus was of the "nothing-but" persuasion. He is that limiting case of all *materialistic* philosophies seeking truth in matter. It was Democritus who teased his contemporaries with the announcement that in reality "There is nothing but atoms and a void." In other words, everything reduces to irreducible and undistinguishable particles and, at that point, nothing can be distinguished from anything else. His views foreshadowed the modern concept of entropy, the maximally probable state of the universe in which an infinity of particles distribute themselves homogeneously in an infinite volume. Order and form, then, are nothing but temporary conditions and abstract inventions. Whereas Socrates and Aristotle would remove the ear of a horse to see how it fit into the design, Democritus smashed the toy. When he was done, the horse was nothing but the air we breathe.

Never since has *atomism* been offered with the severity of Democritus. Reductionism can go no farther. The next step is not philosophy or physics; it is religion. At the base of any materialistic system, however, is the conviction that reality is expressed in matter and that anything with existence has substance. The shortened gospel is this: If a thing exists, it exists in some degree and therefore can be located and measured.

Sciences spring from philosophies as oaks from acorns. Empiricism gave us behaviorism. Idealism spawned the Gestaltists. And philosophical materialism is the parent of physiological psychology.

More specifically, the materialism upon which today's neural sciences are founded is the materialism of René Descartes and the philosophers who followed him. It was Descartes who stated the philosophy in the form necessary for transition into science, although Descartes himself would not have applauded later developments.

## THE MODEST MATERIALISM OF DESCARTES

René Descartes (1596–1650) is portrayed by the great Dutch artist Franz Hals (Figure 1-2) as serious, perhaps a bit rough, almost "on the run." His seriousness is of course documented by an extraordinary record of scientific and philosophical creativity. In regard to roughness, he frequently volunteered eagerly for service as a mercenary soldier. As for the image of him "on the run," he left his native France for Holland—and changed residences two dozen times while in Holland—to escape the distracting attention of his admirers. Descartes was, in short, a man of courage, conviction, energy, and depth.

We will ignore his considerable accomplishments in science and mathematics—his invention of analytical geometry, his studies in physiological optics—and attend to his conservative materialism.[2] Descartes was obsessed by the act of thinking. He would remain in

**FIGURE 1-2**
Portrait of René Descartes by Franz Hals. (Frederick Lewis photo.)

bed for hours, ignoring visitors and friends and food and the light of day, for the sole purpose of reflection. That this habit was not simply disguised sloth is proved beyond doubt by even a casual reading of his *Meditations*.

On first encounter, the famous *Cogito ergo sum* (I think; therefore I am) may appear to be just one more facile homily dropping from the lips of the lazy rationalist. Nothing could be further from the facts.

Descartes was consumed by the question of reality, in particular his own reality. Beyond that, he was taunted by the general question of validity or, more heroically, *truth*. His dilemma rushes out of the Second Meditation: "I will reject . . . whatever admits of the least doubt just as if I had found that it was wholly false; and I will go on until I know something for certain—even if it is only this, that there is nothing certain." In apparent dejection he worries that "whatever things I see are illusions" created by a mendacious mind and a fickle memory. "Well, am I at any rate something?" Here is the crux of it. If he accepts the possibility that all reality is but the deception of his senses, must he also question the validity of his own existence? It is to this question that *Cogito ergo sum* ("I think; therefore, I am") is the answer. For even if there were an evil god committed to driving each of Descartes's perceptions to error, in order for him to be in error he would have to *be*. His consciousness cannot be deceived unless it exists. In the last analysis, then, it is the mind and its workings that establish the validity of existence.

Only after settling this fundamental question could Descartes move on to those matters more directly related to our present business. Given that we *are*, what are the causes of the way we are? At the time Descartes approached this question, the world of scholarship was getting rid of those last cobwebs of the Middle Ages, or what some have called the Age of Faith. Copernicus had set the heavens in order in 1543. Kepler had supplied their laws in 1609, the same year that Galileo was peering through one of the first telescopes and finding more heavenly bodies than the sacred number (seven) would allow. Descartes was thirteen at the time of these discoveries and a very bright thirteen, indeed. His learning was privileged to flower in the world's greatest age of astronomy. The astronomy of Copernicus, Kepler, and Galileo was observational, mathematical, and mechanical, and these features served as models for the mind. Inclined more toward psychological matters, coming as he did from the traditions of philosophy, Descartes attempted to incorporate these models into biological contexts, to establish a mechanistic and (ultimately) mathematical biology. Tangible examples of what he had in mind were everywhere in the gardens and opulent courts of regal France.

Intricate clocks with mobile figures paced off the hours as fluid-driven manikins bowed gracefully when valves opened and others closed. Here, in these toys of an empire, Descartes found the principles of animal behavior—or so he thought. What are the routine actions of man other than the motion of fluids through pipes that flood and drain the organs of movement? With this idea in mind, Descartes proceeded to develop a mechanistic biology and a partly materialistic psychology. Published in the year of his death, *Les Passions de l'ame* sets forth a dualistic view of man, in which the will operates in the service of the soul while all other actions conform to the laws of mechanics. The same evidence that Descartes had used to defend the validity of his own existence was here applied to man, who, unlike all other animals, has a mind in the machine.

**FIGURE 1-3**
Descartes's drawing of "hydraulic" young man. The fire (A) excites the skin of the foot (B) and moves the "fluids" along C-C. These fluids then enter the "pores" of the brain at D and E. Through the marvelous workings of the pineal gland (F) it becomes possible for the foot to be withdrawn, ". . . just as, by pulling one of [the] ends of a string, you make a bell ring that is attached to the other end."

As Figure 1-3 shows, the Cartesian animal is a miracle of hydromechanics. Each small set of muscles is served by a complex of tiny tubules. Flexion is achieved by the filling of flexors and the draining of extensors. (Descartes was well aware of the reciprocal and antagonistic nature of muscular activity.) The fluids or "spirits" in the tubes are directed by external stimuli. Sensations lead to motion in a particular direction to allow appropriate responses. Mediating these two sets of events—sensation and action—is the brain. Receptors are distributed all over the body and within the major sense organs. Impinging stimuli set up in these nerves patterns of vibration that are carried (by the heat of the heart) to the "pores" of the brain. Depending on the nature of the stimulus and its corresponding vibrations, different pores open and close to varying degrees and thus control the pattern of spirit movements to the various muscles. In this way, each soulless little robot moves about the world in a wonderful and orderly fashion.

Man, however, has far more going for him. He has will and consciousness, desire and purpose. He enjoys these faculties by virtue of his immortal soul. The question now is how the soul comes to express its influence upon the machine (the body). There must be, reasoned Descartes, some locus of action, a place where all the mechanical forces converge and from which they can be directed. In his gross observations of the anatomy of the nervous system, he was struck by two findings: that nearly every structure is duplicated symmetrically on each side of the body and that one structure, the pineal gland, is not duplicated. And so the unduplicated structure, the pineal gland, became the locus of action in the Cartesian neuropsychological system. Within this gland, according to Descartes, the soul seeks control of the body. It is here that awareness, intention, and freedom have their source. What a grand part to play for such a little organ.

In Article XXXV of *Les Passions de l'ame,* Descartes gives us an illustration of the chain of events:

Thus, for example, if we see some animal approach us, the light reflected from its body depicts two images of it, one in each of our eyes, and these two images form two others, by means of the optic nerves, in the interior surface of the brain which faces its cavities; then from there, by means of the animal spirits with which its cavities are filled, these images so radiate towards the little gland which is surrounded by these spirits, that the movement which forms each point of one of the images tends towards the same point of the gland towards which tends the movement which forms the point of the other image, which represents the same part of this animal. By this means the two images which are in the brain form but one upon the gland, which, acting immediately upon the soul, causes it to see the form of this animal.

The pineal gland, then, serves as a valve to regulate the flow of spirits that act upon the soul. More complex functions—such as memory, desire, motion, and attention—are explained similarly.

Memory, for example, is but the flow of spirits over the pores of the brain until they find those pores that contain the "traces" of the events the soul desires to recall. Although the machine and the soul interact, the soul is the final arbiter of all psychological events: "The will is so free in its nature that it can never be constrained."

## IMMODEST MATERIALISM

Descartes was the spokesman and the product of a scientific age that was brilliant and energetic but not fully mature. What he had labored to develop took place in a context that was too new, too untested. The products of his inquiries could not go unchallenged for long. Some of the challenges were small but cogent. In 1675 a physiologist named Glisson placed a muscle preparation in water, stimulated the muscle to contract, and observed that it displaced no more water than it had displaced while relaxed. The warranted conclusion was that muscular contractions are not caused by the in-pouring of animal spirits. Other criticisms were more global and therefore more fundamental. These dealt with Descartes's insistence that the soul cannot be brought under the same mechanistic principles as those governing the body. Descartes was devoutly religious and lived in a highly sensitive religious period. He was not frail in the face of authority. Everything we know of him suggests that the theology in his biology was based upon conviction and reason, not timidity or a desire for approval. But even if he had been so inclined, the first half of the seventeenth century was no time to tamper with the soul. Galileo's summons by the Inquisition (1633) was for the much smaller offense of accepting a Copernican universe.

Only as the eighteenth century neared did it become easier politically and ever more necessary scientifically to separate nature from the supernatural. How, for example, could the great Newtonian heavens conform unerringly to the commands of physical law while, in Voltaire's words, there is "a little creature, five feet tall, acting just as he pleases, solely according to his own caprice?" What is gained by introducing the notion of "the soul's desire" in an attempt to account for man's desire? Does it not make more sense, in explaining how we see an animal approaching us, to speak only of images in the eyes, activity in the nerves, and actions of the brain? While philosophers and theologians in this "Age of Reason" may have felt more comfortable avoiding such questions, scientifically oriented scholars found them appealing; for if the very essence of man, his soul, could be reduced or translated to the same materialistic terms as those employed in studies of biology, then all of the machine would be known.

Many figures of the early eighteenth century glanced furtively at the possibility. One man took it as a given. His name was Julien Offray de la Mettrie. In *L'Homme machine* (1748), his maligned and acid treatise, he strikes the death-knell for dualism: "Since all the faculties of the soul depend to such a degree on the proper organization of the brain and of the whole body that apparently they are but this organization itself, the soul is clearly an *enlightened machine.*"

Neuropsychology had been born.

## NOTES AND REFERENCES

1. A brief and readable discussion of these ancient shifts in emphasis may be found in M. T. McClures, "*The Early Philosophers of Greece*" (New York: Appleton-Century, 1935).
2. It cannot be overemphasized that associating the term *materialism* with Descartes demands full qualification. Descartes was a *dualist* and rejected completely the possibility that the spiritual side of man can in any way be understood in materialistic terms. What I try to indicate in the text is that his "modest materialism" permitted an examination of common *behavior* in light of mechanisms. His most materialistic psychology is offered in his posthumously published *Treatise of Man,* which appeared in 1662. Even here, however, Descartes cannot find a *mechanism* able to effect the abstract moral and rational processes common to humanity.

# 2
# The Search for Mechanisms

In an attempt to justify its esoteric searches, science often boasts that technological discoveries are its offspring. But just as frequently, perhaps, developments are reversed. A technical triumph anticipates the scientific principle upon which it is based. There is nothing surprising in this, since it is far easier to *do* things than it is to *know* things. Animals were swimming long before Archimedes suggested the laws of buoyancy, and sailboats were common centuries before aerodynamics. Similarly, the invention of telephones and computers preceded speculations on the "switchboard" and "computerlike" activities of the brain.

Such speculation is characteristic of all sciences in their earlier stages. They are not *analytical;* they are *analogical.* That is, explanations are based not upon demonstrable relationships but upon analogies; they take the form of "*X* is like *Y*" where *X* is something to be explained (e.g., the motion of the sun across the heavens) and *Y* is some easily imagined event (the gods pulling it with horse-drawn chariots). In science, analogies are often called *models.* They are invoked when knowledge of the basic process is lacking.

Descartes observed the movement of mechanical figures and found in this technological marvel a scientific principle by which to account for animal behavior. Since the movements of one are like the actions of the other, he concluded that the underlying processes were the same. The great esteem in which Descartes was held and the influence and importance of his writings set many to work on the problem. Glisson's research has already been mentioned. But although Glisson's findings challenged the notion of fluid forces, they shed no light whatever on the mechanisms that actually do serve behavior. Nearly two centuries elapsed before analogy gave way to insight. Some of the more significant intervening discoveries warrant citation.

## THE SPIRITS

The concept of "spirits" is among the oldest in man's written search for the causes of his own behavior. Among the most significant functions of the soul catalogued by Aristotle was that of *locomotion*. Somehow, the influences of the soul are brought to bear upon the muscles and other organs of activity. Because of their hidden nature, it became popular to describe these psychic forces as "spirits." Those responsible for life were "vital"; those for action, "animal." As early as the thirteenth century, the idea of spirits was prominent in biological theories. We learn this from a charming little book written by Bartholomew Anglicus, who, in less than one hundred pages, summarized all that was known "for certain" in his time: "The vital spirit [responsible for life] is spread into all the body and worketh in the artery veins the pulses of life. . . . [The] animal spirit [responsible for action] is gendered in the foremost den of the brain, and is somewhat spread into the limbs of feeling." The spirits, however, are not entirely used up on feeling and motion: "Some part thereof abideth in the aforesaid dens, that common sense, the common wit, and the virtue imaginative may be made perfect."

Bartholomew tells us that different names are given to the spirits to distinguish their various functions. He also warns us that the soul requires such mechanisms to accomplish its work but that the mechanisms are not the soul itself: "One and the same spirit is named by divers names. For by working in the liver it is called the natural spirit, in the heart the vital spirit, and in the head the animal spirit. We may not believe that this spirit is man's reasonable soul, but more soothly, as saith Austin, the car thereof and proper instrument . . . without the service of such a spirit, no act the soul may perfectly exercise in the body."

Bartholomew labored long before the dawn of modern science and was under no burden of proof other than that of reasoned argument. By the seventeenth century, matters had changed. Experimentalism was in the air, and the scientific theorist didn't have long to wait between the publication of his notions and tests of them by some independent worker. It wasn't until the nineteenth century that the dominant flavor of science would be frantically experimental, but by

Descartes's time there were enough empiricists to form a band, if not an orchestra. The orchestra began to assemble with la Mettrie's "enlightened machine" (1748) and with the research of Robert Whytt, published in 1751.

## NERVOUS POWER

Whytt had the advantage of a century's work separating his efforts from Descartes's foundations. Good anatomical studies had furthered knowledge of where the nerves are located and how they interconnect. Physiologists were busy with their dissections, an effort that reached one major plateau with William Harvey's discovery (1749) of the circulation of the blood. By Whytt's time, many were engaged in studies of the structures of the nervous system. He found that he could produce movement by stimulating the spinal cord. Pricking it led to the contraction of muscles even when the local blood supply was eliminated: "While the nervous power is immediately necessary to muscular motion, the arterial blood seems to act only in a secondary or more remote manner."

In other words, it was not necessary to account for motion in terms of substances carried by the blood. Indeed, Whytt was most prudent in the matter of naming the agent of action: "The immediate cause of muscular contraction, which, from what has been said, appears evidently to be lodged in the brain and nerves, I choose to distinguish by the terms of the *power* or *influence of the nerves;* and if, in compliance with custom, I shall at any time give it the name of *animal* or *vital spirits,* I desire it may be understood to be without any view of ascertaining its particular nature or manner of acting."

Whytt demonstrated also the antagonistic pairing of the muscles, by which the contraction of one is achieved only with the relaxation of its partner. The significance of this—beyond the mere fact—was that the motions are controllable by local arrangements and do not require the intervention of the mind (soul). Thus, physiologically, Whytt provided evidence for involuntary behavior, or what we commonly call *reflexes.* He achieved all this without relying upon spirits. In fact, as he states unapologetically, the particular nature of the responsible mechanism is simply not known.

In 1784, Prochaska ignored the spirits entirely and discussed reflexes in terms of a *vis nervosa,* a nervous force. He boasted that *"we abandon the Cartesian method of philosophizing in this part of animal physics also, and adopt the Newtonian"* as he completed the materialistic portrait of behavior. One of the most prophetic items in his treatise concerns the precise nature of the *vis nervosa: "Vis nervosa* is as divisible as the nervous system, so that it remains in each portion of a bisected nerve. . . . Nor does the *vis nervosa* of the nerves require continual supplies from the brain, since nerves possess their own."

Quite a development! From animal spirits heated by the passions of the heart and cooled in the dens of the brain to a physical substance; from the spirits of the nervous tubules and the valves in the pineal gland to the notion of a force implicit in neural tissue itself. And then, within five years of Prochaska's publication, Luigi Galvani goes shopping for supper and returns to fashion an idea that at once rids science of the spirits and at the same time provides a modern mechanism to power the enlightened machine.

## THE NERVE IMPULSE

In an account that may well be apocryphal, Luigi Galvani (1737–1798) is supposed to have returned from the market with a bag of freshly killed frogs. Preparing them for dinner under his wife's careful supervision, he hung them from wire perches and performed the necessary surgery by placing each frog on a metal table. He finished one frog. Then, with one hand on the metal counter, he reached back with the other to grab another frog—and the legs of the hanging frogs began to twitch.

Although no one will guarantee the veracity of the account, it is known that Galvani undertook a series of experiments involving many of these same steps (see Figure 2-1). In Galvani's experiments, the frog's leg was fastened to a brass hook that penetrated the massive muscles of the thigh. The foot of the frog, when at rest, dropped to make contact with a silver strip. Each time the foot touched the strip, the muscle contracted, withdrawing the leg and thus breaking the circuit. With the stimulus removed, the leg once again fell, the circuit was closed, and the leg flexed again. Galvani, who unknowingly had just invented the wet-cell battery, understandably concluded that the *vis nervosa* is electrical. And, indeed it is, but not for the reasons available to Galvani.

Galvani's whole argument came under a cloud of suspicion in 1800, when a much better physicist, Alessandro Volta (1745–1827), repeated the "frog effect," using only discs of different metal separated by cardboard sheets soaked in brine. This "Voltaic pile," the forerunner of the modern wet-cell battery, demonstrated that current will flow between different metal conductors if a good conducting medium is placed between. Galvani's frog, then, functioned exactly like a cardboard disc soaked in saline.

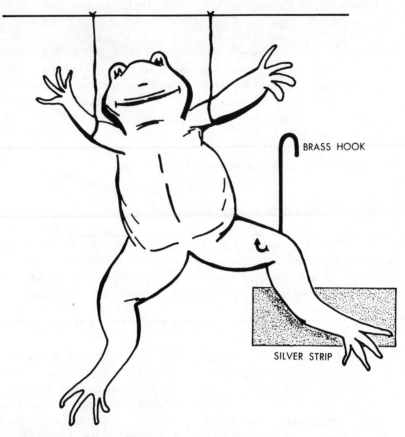

**BRASS HOOK**

**SILVER STRIP**

*FIGURE 2-1*
Sketch of Luigi Galvani's experiment on the nervous impulse in frogs.

Through the efforts of Galvani and Volta, it became possible to construct a device that would measure this flow of electrons, a device named the *galvanometer*—which shows that one need not be right to be respected. With this instrument, it was soon demonstrated that electrical energy is a property of living tissue and does not have to get into tissue from some other source. In the earliest experiments, a needle was inserted into muscle, another was placed on electrically neutral substances, and the galvanometer bridged these two probes. The recorded electrical flow was called the *current of injury* on the theory that only damaged tissue so responded. It was quickly learned, however, that injury is not a necessary condition. Resting tissue contains an *intrinsic* electricity. For muscles to contract, these electrical events must travel down the nerves and directly stimulate the muscle tissue.

Even in the nineteenth century, the vestiges of Cartesian biology were visible. Many continued to believe that the agencies of the soul—whether they were "spirits," "vis nervosa," or "electrons"—had their effects upon the body immediately. The notion had the support not only of authority and theology but of common sense as well; for, clearly, no time elapses between our willing to do something and our doing it. But as the middle of the nineteenth century approached, even this memento of the "old order" was dissolved. The great Helmholtz, with the advantages of a new technology, measured the speed of neural conduction and found it to be only about 40 meters per second, about 85 miles per hour. How humble a number when compared with the estimates that had preceded it—estimates varying between instantaneous and values that were multiples of the velocity of light. With this measurement, the mind seemed to lose much of the mystery that had kept it outside the laboratory. Not only was its mechanism of action known and measurable; it was modest as well. The "spirits" were real and, as la Mettrie had warned, were in the province not of philosophy or religion but of physics.[1]

The modern theory of the nerve impulse begins with the *neuron*, the unit of the nervous system. It wasn't until a half-century ago, through the work of S. Ramon y Cajal, that there was proof of separate neural units. Until the advent of high-power microscopes, many continued to believe, with Descartes, that the nervous system was a collection of continuous tubes, breaking up into smaller and smaller filaments.

Neurons come in different sizes and shapes, so that any sketch of a "typical" neuron, including the one shown in Figure 2-2, is misleading. Generally, however, there is a region of the cell especially equipped to make contact with preceding neurons. These contact points are called *dendrites*. The body of the cell, its *soma*, contains a nucleus and other structures such as the *mitochondria*, which participate in the metabolic aspects of the neuron's activity. Then, there is a (typically) long process, sometimes two of them, along which the neural *impulse* travels. This process is called the *axon*. Every region of the neuron reveals electrical properties, but *impulses* generally occur only in the axon (although they can also be found in the long dendrites of certain sensory neurons).

If we examine a single axon, we find that its membranous covering separates the components of the axon (i.e., the *axoplasm*) from a surrounding medium that is different in composition. The axoplasm

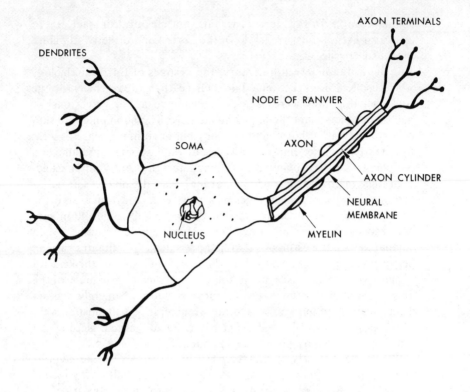

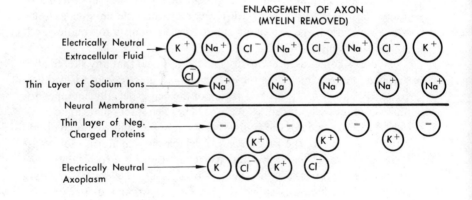

ENLARGEMENT OF AXON
(MYELIN REMOVED)

Electrically Neutral
Extracellular Fluid

Thin Layer of Sodium Ions

Neural Membrane

Thin layer of Neg.
Charged Proteins

Electrically Neutral
Axoplasm

**FIGURE 2-2**
The neuron and expanded axon showing chemical constituents.

contains an abundance of potassium but relatively little sodium. The surrounding medium (the extracellular space) reveals a high concentration of sodium but relatively little potassium. The axoplasm also contains large protein "ions" not found in the same concentration outside the axon. All these materials—sodium, potassium, protein— exist in *ionic* form; that is, as atoms (or, in the case of the proteins, as molecules) with either an abundance or a deficiency of electrons. In other words, they are electrically *charged* in that they will seek to gain or relinquish electrons in order to attain a state of electrical neutrality. Because the sodium and potassium ions each lack a single electron, they are said to be positively charged (+). The protein "ions" will bind to any atom needing two electrons, since the proteins have an excess of two (i.e., a negative charge of – – ).

Under ordinary circumstances, whenever a region of electrical charge is separated from one of a different charge, the ions or electrons will flow until an equilibrium is established. That is why a battery provides electricity. Moreover, whenever there is a difference in concentration between two adjacent regions, ions will flow in order to establish an ionic equilibrium. In other words, under ordinary conditions, two forces would work to change the electrical and chemical features of the axon: (1) Sodium ions would enter and potassium ions would leave the axoplasm until the concentration of each ion is the same within the axoplasm as it is outside. (2) The internal negativity produced by the excess of negatively charged protein ions would be offset either by the movement of the proteins from the axoplasm out to the surrounding medium or by the flow of external positive ions into the axoplasm.

However, *ordinary* conditions do not obtain where the axon is concerned. First of all, the axon is covered by a membrane that does not allow the flow of ions through it to occur willy-nilly. The protein ions are simply too large to pass through the spaces in the membrane. Moreover, since sodium ions line the outside of the membrane and potassium ions the inside, these two like-charged ions tend to repel each other, further limiting the establishment of an ionic equilibrium. (See Figure 2-3.) Thus, electrical forces act in opposition to an ionic equilibrium, and the *semipermeable* nature of the membrane works against the establishment of an equal distribution of charges. Finally, for reasons that are as yet unclear, the membrane in its resting state is less permeable to the entrance of sodium than it is to the exit of potassium.

Somehow these various tensions resolve themselves. An unsteady peace exists between the membrane and the fluids on either side of it. The physical value of this armistice is called the *resting membrane*

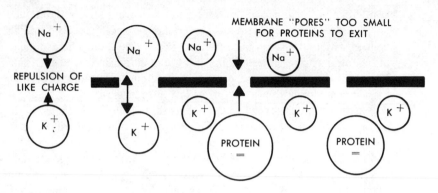

FIGURE 2-3

*potential.*[2] Each word in this term describes a different feature: *resting* because these various conditions exist only while the axon is unstimulated; *membrane* effect because only the membrane's ability to hold a charge across it allows the disequilibrium to be maintained. Finally, it is a *potential* because, as a system in electrical disequilibrium, the *potential* for ion flow is ever present. Some of these characteristics can be demonstrated rather simply. A solution of postassium chloride can be mixed with casein, which is a milk derivative and which ionizes into large protein ions. The whole solution can be placed inside a semipermeable membrane, such as a bladder, and immersed in a beaker of a neutral solution of sodium chloride. If we measure the "charge" across the membrane in air (relatively uncharged) before immersing the membrane and its contents, we find that none exists. Similarly, by definition, a *neutral* solution of sodium chloride also lacks charge. However, once the bladder is placed within the NaCl, the picture changes. The casein cannot flow out. Thus, more negative charge is kept within the bladder than there is outside. If we use a modern and more sensitive galvanometer to bridge wires placed on the outside of the bladder and within the bladder's contents, we shall record a voltage. We can eliminate it by adding a negatively charged ion to the NaCl solution or by adding more potassium to the contents of the bladder.

Similar but far more difficult experiments have been done with axons. Figure 2-4 shows one such experiment. A very finely drawn glass tube is inserted into the axoplasm from the cut end of the axon. The tube is filled with a conducting material.[3] Another electrode is placed on the surface of the axon's membrane. A sensitive voltmeter measures the resting membrane potential as about seventy thousandths of a volt; that is, 70 millivolts (mv). Of course, very few axons

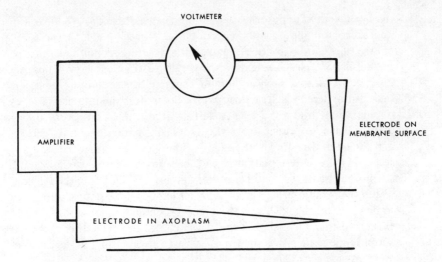

*FIGURE 2-4*
Schematic diagram describing procedure for measuring neural impulse.

are large enough to allow this experiment. The squid has one (its *giant axon*) that is about a millimeter in diameter; for this reason, many a squid has advanced the cause of neurophysiology. But just about the same results can be obtained from recordings taken from the whole nerve; that is, from a collection of axons. (The term *nerve*, technically, refers not to a neuron but to a band of axons running together.) When one electrode is inserted into the nerve and another is placed on its surface, a resting potential can also be measured. The same effect is obtained when one electrode is inserted into the nerve bundle and another is placed on some indifferent (electrically neutral) point such as an earlobe or a toe. Again, the inside of the structure is found to be negatively charged and the potential is of the order of – 70 mv.

Once a stimulus is applied, everything becomes transformed into a majestic chaos. Somehow, with the presentation of a stimulus—an electrical pulse, a mechanical "prick," heat, nearly anything—the membrane momentarily breaks down, sodium rushes into the axoplasm, potassium is pushed out, and the potential difference across the membrane is liquidated. In fact, at the height of activity, the axoplasm actually becomes *positively* charged relative to the outside. Nor do these alterations mount gradually. At one instant, the resting potential dominates. Then, with ever so slight an increase in stimulus strength, the *threshold* is just exceeded, and ions flow with full force. It is no wonder that the event is referred to as an "impulse" or that the law invented to describe it should be called "the *all-or-none law* of neural conduction." The neuron either "fires" or it doesn't. Of course, if it is ever to "fire" again, initial (resting) conditions must be reestablished. They are established, but it isn't clear how. Thus, we must rely tentatively on a "demon" named "the sodium pump." The task of the demon is straightforward. Soon after the impulse reaches its peak magnitude, the events that created it must be reversed. Sodium must be extruded from the axoplasm, potassium must return, and the overall resting potential of − 70 mv must be restored. Indeed, sodium is slowly pumped out, as we can prove; that is, we can "tag" sodium ions with radioactive material and, in geiger counter fashion, watch the sodium being removed. As it happens, the potassium leaves somewhat more slowly than a corresponding amount of sodium enters, so that for a short time at the end of the cycle the interior is actually more negative than it is at rest (always relative to the medium outside the axoplasm).

As Figure 2-5 shows, the entire chain of events takes about six

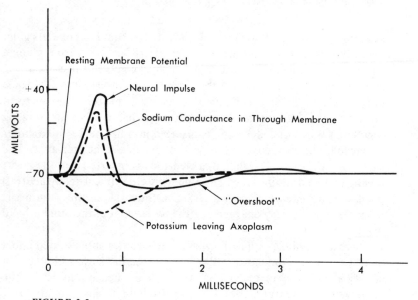

**FIGURE 2-5**

The neural impulse. The impulse is established as sodium rushes in from the extracellular medium and potassium is extruded from the axoplasmic medium. Note that potassium ions take longer to return to their initial conductances than sodium ions. Thus, there is a time following the peak of the impulse when there is less $K^+$ within the membrane than is the case in the resting state. This is the major reason for the negative "overshoot" in the waveform of the neural impulse.

thousandths of a second, or 6 milliseconds (msec). The vertical values (those on the ordinate) are measures of the potential difference in millivolts between the axoplasm and the surrounding medium. The value at rest is − 70 mv. With the arrival of a stimulus, and after a brief latency, the value becomes progressively more positive, passing through 0 mv and reaching a peak of about +50 mv. Then the charge reverses, passing again through 0, down past − 70 mv, and then back up to the resting level. Figure 2-5 also shows the relative concentrations of sodium and potassium in the axoplasm during each phase of the neural impulse. The electrical features of the impulse are simply derived from the flow of these ions.

The impulse is either initiated or it is not; when it is, it occurs at full strength. Life may be filled with equivocation and indecision, but axons are not. So single-minded are they that while they are responding and for a short time after, they will answer no other call. At the immediate conclusion of an impulse, there is no stimulus strong enough to elicit another. During this time, the neuron is said to be in an *absolute refractory period*, which lasts about 1 msec. Then, for another millisecond or so, only a very strong stimulus—one considerably greater than that demanded by the resting neuron—will succeed in initiating an impulse. This phase is called the *relative refractory period*.

In saying that the membrane of the resting neuron separates media of differing ionic concentrations and charge, we are saying that, as with a magnet, there are (relatively) positive and negative *poles*. It is conventional, therefore, to describe the initiation of an impulse as the outcome of *depolarization* (destruction of the polar tension). Anything that increases the potential difference across the membrane leads, then, to a state of *hyperpolarization*. The hyperpolarized membrane will have a higher threshold. That is, more of a stimulus will be needed to produce an impulse than would be required in the normally polarized state. Similarly, anything that diminishes the resting potential creates a state of *hypopolarization*.

Some methods of inducing hyperpolarization and hypopolarization should be obvious. For example, the composition of the extracellular fluids can be altered by the addition of more sodium (hyperpolarization) or negatively charged ions (hypopolarization). Or a *subthreshold* stimulus, one too weak to initiate the impulse but strong enough to "prime the pump," can be applied. Under this condition, less of a subsequent stimulus is needed to initiate the impulse. Of course, once it is initiated, its properties are independent of this prior "conditioning." But when the chemical medium of the axoplasm or the surrounding fluids is altered, the amplitude of the impulse is changed dramatically.

For example, if the sodium concentration difference is reduced, the resulting impulse will be reduced.

The resting potential and the neural impulse must be understood as outcomes of different processes. We can predict the resting membrane potential very accurately by ignoring everything except the concentration differences of potassium on either side of the membrane. These differences, if they occurred in a simple battery, would result in a "charge" of about $-75$ mv (inside vs. outside), a value close to the obtained $-70$ mv. However, the concentration differences of sodium lead to a very different value, $+50$ mv. That is, if in our calculation of a predicted resting potential we considered only the amount of sodium on each side of the membrane, we would arrive at the value of $+50$ mv. Interestingly, although this value is gravely in error as a measure of the *resting* potential, it is the exact value of the maximum amplitude of the neural *impulse*. These calculations have spawned several careful and ingenious experiments which confirm our suspicions. The resting potential is due almost exclusively to potassium differences, while the impulse is entirely in the province of sodium. When we alter sodium concentrations, we influence the impulse but not the resting potential. When we tamper with potassium concentrations, we change the resting potential but have little effect upon the impulse. (See Figure 2-6.)

### Saltatory Conduction

The sketch of the neuron offered earlier (Figure 2-2) shows the axon covered with a sheath that is discontinuous. Most mamalian neurons have this covering. It is called *myelin* and is composed mostly of cholesterol and fatty acids. The "breaks" occur about every millimeter and are called *Nodes of Ranvier,* after their discoverer. At the nodes, the membrane is in contact with the surrounding medium; between nodes, it is insulated from the surroundings. Conduction of impulses by these myelinated axons has been found to be from node to node. Impulse activity is not observed along the internodal distance. Thus, the impulse "skips" down the axon. This type of conduction has therefore been named *saltatory* (from the Latin *salto,* skip). In the absence of myelin, conduction is analogous to a flame journeying down a wick, lighting each successive region to the same degree.[4]

### The Synapse

The dendrites of a neuron do not make physical contact with the axonal filaments of the preceding neuron. There is a small space between, referred to as the *synapse.* Present knowledge of the

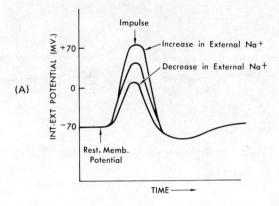

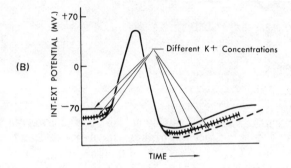

**FIGURE 2-6**
Resting potential and the neural impulse. (A) Sodium concentration determines amplitude of impulse but does not influence either resting potential or late negative over-shoot. (B) Potassium concentration influences resting and late negative potentials but not amplitude of impulse.

synapse is limited but growing.[5] What appears to happen is this: As the impulse arrives at the small terminal branches of the axon, it causes little pouches or vesicles to secrete a substance into the synaptic space. The substance migrates across the synapse and stimulates the dendritic branches on the other side. These branches, however, are not capable of initiating impulses. Instead, they change in *graded* fashion. That is, they provide a small response when contacted by a small amount of the *transmitter* substance and a progressively larger response as the amount of transmitter increases. (See Figure 2-7.)

There are several reasons for postulating a *chemical* means of transmission across the synapse. Microscopic studies indicate that

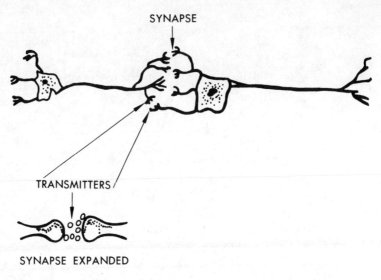

SYNAPSE

TRANSMITTERS

SYNAPSE EXPANDED

**FIGURE 2-7**
The synapse.

the distance between the terminal fibers of the presynaptic neuron and the dendritic processes of the postsynaptic neuron is about 200 Å (an angstrom [Å] is one ten millionth of a meter). We know also that the time between presynaptic electrical activity and postsynaptic electrical activity is of the order of 200–300 millionths of a second. If, instead of chemical induction, the postsynaptic response were electrically induced, it would occur much more quickly; that is, electrical induction would cross a 200-A space in less than 200 millionths of a second. Furthermore, we can record both inhibitory and excitatory postsynaptic signals from the *same* neuron. These different electrical events would not be expected if the postsynaptic event were but the reflection of a presynaptic *electrical* signal. Yet such effects could be produced if the synaptic space were flooded with different transmitter substances. Finally, given the strength of the presynaptic potential, we can predict what the amplitude of the postsynaptic response should be if the latter were simply induced electrically by the former. As it happens, the postsynaptic response is far greater than what is predicted by the assumption of electrical induction. All told, the need for a chemical mechanism is great if a theory of synaptic transmission is to account for what is already known about trans-synaptic events.

Some axons terminate not on dendrites but on cell bodies. That is, the connection is not axo-dendritic but axo-somatic. Here too there is a synaptic space across which the transmitter substances must migrate. As with dendrites, the soma cannot respond impulsively, but only in graded fashion. However, once the graded activity reaches some threshold value, the axon responds with a neural impulse. The chain of events is as follows: (1) neural impulse in the axon of neuron 1, (2) secretion of transmitter substances when the impulse reaches the terminal branches of neuron 1, (3) migration of the transmitters across the synaptic space, (4) graded responses of the dendrites or cell body of neuron 2 when stimulated by the transmitter substances, (5) graded responses reaching an amplitude of sufficient strength to initiate impulse activity in the axon of neuron 2.

There still is no clear evidence on the nature of transmitter substances between neurons; where axons enter muscle fibers, however, the synaptic transmitter is *acetylcholine*. Furthermore, when substances known to neutralize chemicals such as acetylcholine are injected near synaptic junctions, conduction in the successive neurons ceases. In fact, one such substance—called acetylcholinesterase—is produced by the successive neurons in order to terminate transmission. The postsynaptic dendrites, after they have been stimulated by the transmitter substances for some critical period of time or to some critical degree, apparently release an inhibitor into the synapse; this inhibitor either directly prevents the formation of transmitters by the preceding axon filaments or it neutralizes the transmitters so formed.

There must be a variety of transmitter substances and their chemical antagonists. In some instances, for example, activity in neuron 1 hyperpolarizes the next unit in the chain (neuron 2) and renders it less responsive to stimulation. This phenomenon is called *postsynaptic inhibitory potential* or *inhibitory postsynaptic potential* (IPSP). In other instances, the effect of 1 on 2 is one of excitation, rendering the next neuron *more* responsive to stimulation. The electrical correlate of this is an *excitatory postsynaptic potential* (EPSP).

Since the language of the nervous system is the neural impulse, an all-or-none event, our experiences and our actions could have none of their fluidity, continuity, and commendable subtlety were it not for synaptic junctions and the EPSPs and IPSPs created at these junctions. At each synapse, the original signal can be either re-created exactly, reduced in amplitude, increased in amplitude, held up briefly, or various combinations of these before being sent along. Moreover, signals from different structures may thus be added or subtracted, multiplied or divided, or transformed into a variety of combinations.

Well, this is something more than Descartes had in mind. Even la

Mettrie, who insisted that our complexity is really the result of the number of parts in the "clock" rather than some invisible force, would have to be impressed with the facts of neurophysiology. But the task has only just begun; for, even though we seem to have found a mechanism, we still have to find out what it's up to. We must explore where these impulses go and how they respond not to the glass electrodes of the physiologist but to the sunsets and clever stories of which human experience is made. To this point, the materialists have told us only that something under our skin can bring the world to us and us through it. But surely the neuron doesn't "know" that that's Socrates, even when he's standing on his head. It isn't the impulse that calls to say we'll be late. We have, to use a metaphor, a vehicle but no map. Some anatomy will help.

## NOTES AND REFERENCES

1. We can understand the excitement created by these findings. We can even have some compassion for those who, in their excitement, believed their discoveries to have some bearing on philosophical matters. Yet, who would have doubted that biological processes have something to do with behavior? And this, after all, is all that was discovered. Even Descartes would have expected as much; indeed, he speculated as much. We find some of the same enthusiasm in modern times generated by inventions such as the telephone and the computer. In the 1940s, the human nervous system was a gigantic "switchboard"; in the 1950s, a computer. Such statements show a carelessness with language and, over the long haul, retard the evolution of useful explanatory devices.

2. The classical papers on the resting membrane potential and the action potential are those of D. R. Curtis and K. S. Cole: *J. cell. comp. Physiol.*, 1942, *19*, 135–144; A. L. Hodgkin and A. F. Huxley: *Nature*, 1939, *144*, 710–711; A. L. Hodgkin, A. F. Huxley, and B. Katz: *Arch. sci. physiol.*, 1949, *3*, 129–150. An excellent summary of the ionic theory of impulse initiation and conduction is provided by Hodgkin in *Science*, 1964, *145*, 1148–1154. Also recommended highly is his short book, *The Conduction of the Nervous Impulse*, (Springfield, Ill.: Charles Thomas, 1968).

3. See especially Hodgkin, Huxley, and Katz, *J. Physiol.*, 1952, *116*, 424–448. In this paper, the voltage-clamp technique is described.

4. I. Tasaki has summarized his pioneering studies of saltatory con-

duction in *Nervous Transmission* (Springfield, Ill.: Charles Thomas, 1953).

5. Sir John Eccles, who received the Nobel Prize for his research on the synapse, proposed his theory in nearly complete form in 1946 (*Ann. N. Y. Acad. Sci.*, 1946, *47*, 429–455). He reviews two decades of his research in *The Physiology of Synapses*, (New York: Academic Press, 1964).

# 3
# Neural Maps

Today, it is common to hear the neural scientist describe the brain and the rest of the nervous system as "simply a network designed to sense, interpret, and respond." And those who ask about creation, intuition, imagination are likely to be told that, "fundamentally," these are really only "semantic" problems; that once we clean up our language so that we can agree on what we mean by such terms, they too will succumb to the rigor and precision of modern science.

It would be neither fair nor prudent to reject such a promise out of hand. It is often proffered by men of accomplishment, and the best stance by far is to hear them out, look at the facts, and then judge the merits of the prophesy. In fact, even if the science cannot shed much light on those aspects of life that are of greatest interest, it would be no mean feat just to explain how we *sense, interpret,* and *respond.* To begin, we must get at least a general idea of how the nervous system is organized. Its architecture is Byzantine. There are many entrances, and one's view of the entire structure depends upon the point from which it is viewed.

## ANATOMICAL FEATURES OF SENSORY SYSTEMS

### Receptors

The universe is matter and energy. Our experiences must be fashioned from these. Unfortunately, however, most of the matter and energy of the universe is not accessible to us. It is either too far away or, in the case of energy, it arrives in a form that is not compatible with our sense organs. Our private visions, sounds, smells, tastes, and touches are but mist over those oceans of activity that comprise the physical world around us. In order to enjoy even these experiences, we must have specialized cells capable of taking energy in whatever form and, somehow, translating it into the language of the nervous system—*electricity*. The cells that perform this function are called *receptors*, and the function is called, appropriately, *transduction*. A transducer is any device that responds to energy in one form with a reaction in a different form. For example, when light (electromagnetic energy) strikes the surface of a photocell in our front yard, the cell responds with an electrical signal that turns off the lamp on the front porch. With such a device, we can keep the porch lit while the sun is down and turn it off at dawn. The photocell is called a *photoelectric* transducer; it takes photic energy and translates it into electrical energy. Similarly, we can use a metal strip as a *thermomechanical* transducer. When we heat it, it expands, closes an electrical contact, and, for example, turns on the air conditioner. In this case, thermal energy has been converted into a mechanical action. The metal has responded to heat with a mechanical reaction.

Our receptors (see Figure 3-1) perform analogous functions but with an efficiency and a sensitivity unmatched in the world of gadgets. In vision, the receptors (transducers) are specialized cells lining the retina. Because of their general appearance, they are called *rods* and *cones*. Each one—and there are about 120,000,000 rods and 6,000,000 cones—contains a tiny drop of a chemical, distributed over a portion of its surface. When light strikes this substance, it undergoes a decomposition, a kind of "bleaching" analogous to the response of photographic pigments when struck by light. Through a process not yet understood, this decomposition leads to the generation of a small electrical signal in the tail of the receptor. The size of this electrical response depends upon the speed with which the decomposition proceeds; the speed of decomposition depends in part upon the intensity of the incident light and upon the amount of pigment present when the light arrives. So the rods and cones are photochemical transducers and, at the same time, chemoelectrical transducers: they respond chemically to light and then electrically to the chemical change.

A rather different receptor mechanism participates in the sense of hearing. Sound stimuli are mechanical. They are produced by the vibration of molecules in air or in other conducting (elastic) media. These molecular vibrations impinge directly upon the eardrum and cause it to vibrate at the same frequency. The drum is so thin and so

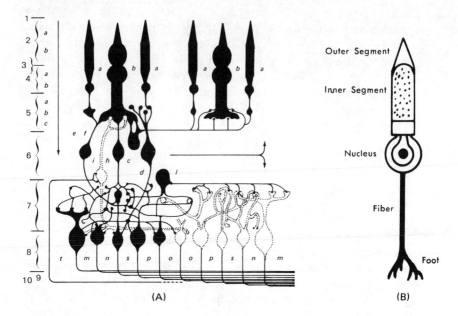

(A)                                                    (B)

**FIGURE 3-1**

Visual and auditory receptors. (A) Cross-section of the retina. The numbers on the left indicate different layers of the retina. The arrows indicate the direction in which the nerve impulse travels. The rods (a) and cones (b) transmit their excitation through the various kinds of bipolar cells (d, e, f, h, i), sometimes across the retina through horizontal cells (c, l), to the ganglion cells (m, n, s, p, o), and on through the optic nerve (layers 9, 10) to the optic nuclei and the visual cortex. (Adapted from S. L. Polyak *The Retina*. Chicago: University of Chicago Press, 1941.) (B) Retinal cone; outer segment and photopigments. Retinal cones have diameters of between 1 and 2 microns (millionths of a meter) and lengths of some 20 to 70 microns. (C) Schematic representation of basilar membrane within the fluids of the cochlear duct. Oscillations in the bones of the middle ear (hammer, anvil, and stirrup) are translated through the oval window to the fluids of the inner ear. Undulations of the basilar membrane result. (Adapted from G. von Békésy [1935], Über Akustische Reizung des Vestibularapparates. *Pfluger Arch. Ges. Physiol. 236,* 59–76.) (D) Structures of the inner ear. Note hair cells extending from the basilar membrane to the tectorial membrane. Fluid vibrations in *scala tympani* (the chamber in which the hair cells reside) induce motion in the basilar membrane. The hair cells are thus placed under tension and respond electrically to this tension. Impulses are then initiated in the nerve fibers which pass into the brain as a bundle, the *auditory nerve*. (Adapted from H. Davis, et al. [1953], Acoustic Trauma in Guinea Pig. *Journal of the Acoustical Society of America, 25,* 1180–1189.)

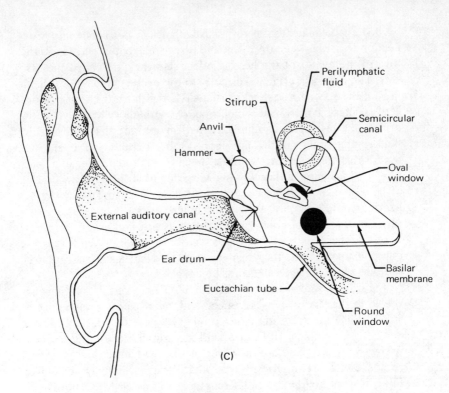

(C)

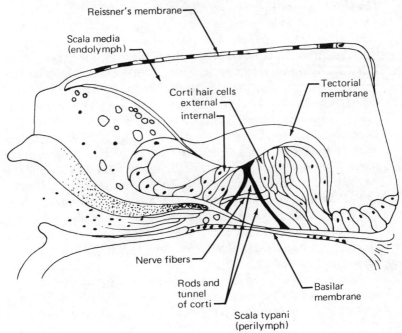

(D)

exquisitely balanced that it responds with nearly perfect fidelity. Connections exist between the drum and three small bones placed inward, toward the center of the head. Collectively they are called the *ossicles*. The first one, attached directly to the drum, is the *incus* ("hammer"); the second, the *malleus* ("anvil"); the third, the *stapes* ("stirrup"). These bones beat synchronously with the vibrations of the drum. The last bone straddles a small membrane that leads to the fluid compartments of the inner ear. As the stirrup moves in and out, it pulls this membranous "window" in and out, in something of a "suction cup" fashion. In this way, the vibration of air leads to a vibration of bone, which leads to a vibration of fluid. Then the receptors for hearing come into play. Within the inner ear, strung across a structure called the *basilar membrane,* are many tiny *hair cells*. Their marvelous property is this: when they are deformed or when forces are imposed upon them, they respond with an electrical signal; that is, they are *mechanoelectrical* transducers.

Figure 3-2 shows some of the other types of receptors, those involved in the "skin" senses (touch, cold, heat, pain), in taste, and in smell. While there is a great variation in shape and size, they all have one thing in common. If they respond to a stimulus at all, the response is *electrical*. They are not, however, *neurons* because their electrical responses are not impulses. Recall what the neural impulse looks like. First, it occurs either at full strength or not at all (the "all-or-none law"). Receptors, in contrast, respond in *graded* fashion, the way dendrites do. And, in fact, dendrites are receptors of a sort. They are certainly transducers in that they respond electrically to the chemical stimulation of the synaptic transmitters. Second, the neural impulse is *nondecremental*. Its amplitude is constant down the entire length of the axon. Here, too, the receptors differ. The further their little signals wander, the weaker they get. Once a neural impulse is initiated, it runs its course, but the electrical response of the receptor ends when the stimulus ends. Finally, and as a result of what has just been said, the effects of quickly arriving stimuli on receptors are additive. The nerve impulse occurs or it does not. But with receptors we can put in a little stimulation, get a little response, add a little more, and get a little more. At some point, when the receptor's response has reached a critical value, the neuron with which the receptor is associated "fires." Thus, the graded ("analogue") response of the receptor is a necessary condition for the impulsive ("digital") response of the neuron.

Receptors and neurons may connect directly or through other structures. In vision, for example, the rods and cones do not make contact with the neurons that comprise the optic nerve. Instead, the

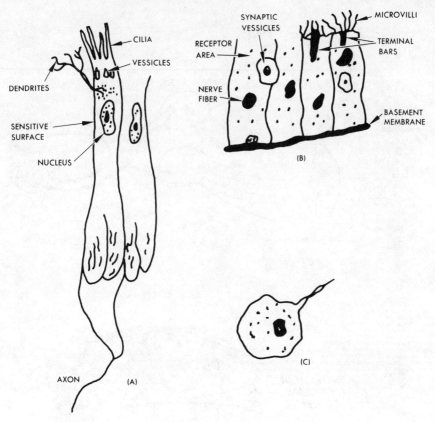

**FIGURE 3-2**
Receptors involved in skin senses, taste, and smell. (A) Olfactory receptor
(schematic). (B) Rabbit taste buds. (C) End bulb of krause: a possible "cold"
receptor in skin.

receptors feed into *bipolar cells,* and these, in turn, activate the optic
nerve fibers. Moreover, layers of horizontally distributed cells also
participate (as shown in Figure 3-3), so that a truly mind-boggling
assortment of possibilities exists in the processing of retinal signals.

### Sensory Neurons

The sensory neurons are responsible for bringing impulses to the
*central nervous system* (CNS). By CNS we mean the brain and the
spinal cord. All neural units that are not part of the CNS comprise
what is known as the *peripheral nervous system* (PNS). A third major

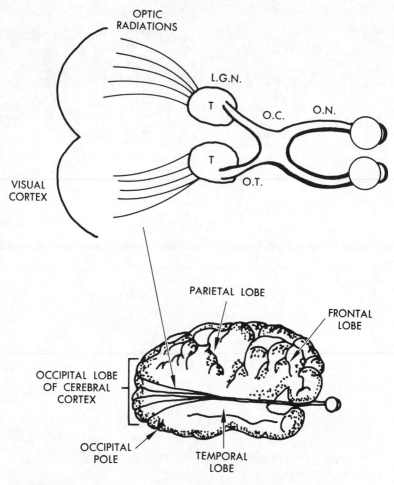

**FIGURE 3-3**
Visual pathways. (O.N., optic nerve; O.C., optic chiasma; O.T., optic tract; L.G.N., lateral geniculate nucleus of thalamus, T.)

division of labor in the nervous system involves neurons that allow communication between the CNS and the smooth muscles (blood vessel muscles, gastric muscles, etc.) and glands (adrenals, thyroid, etc.) of the body. This third system is called the *autonomic nervous system* (ANS) (see Figure 3-4); as we shall see, the ANS plays a significant part in psychological events called "emotional."

It is via the sensory neurons of the PNS and ANS that information from the receptors is delivered to the CNS. The word *afferent*—from the latin word for "bring," "carry," or "bear" (*ferro*) and the prep-

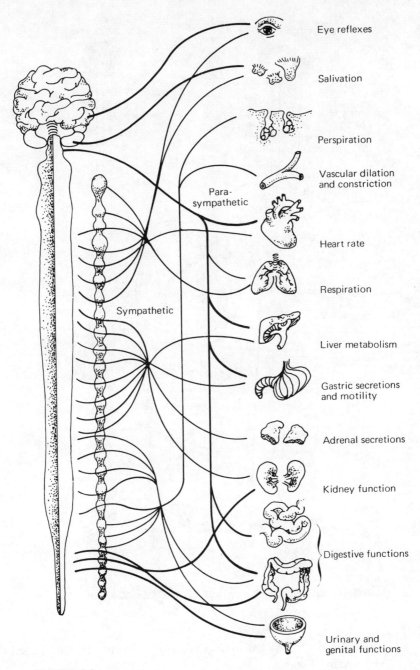

Eye reflexes

Salivation

Perspiration

Vascular dilation
and constriction

Para-
sympathetic

Heart rate

Respiration

Sympathetic

Liver metabolism

Gastric secretions
and motility

Adrenal secretions

Kidney function

Digestive functions

Urinary and
genital functions

**FIGURE 3-4**
Sympathetic and parasympathetic branches of the autonomic nervous system.
Note the long, direct connections between parasympathetic fibers and their
organs of destination. The sympathetic fibers terminate in synapses soon after
leaving the sympathetic ganglia. During states of stress, anxiety, and excitement, all of the functions indicated are affected by autonomic influences.

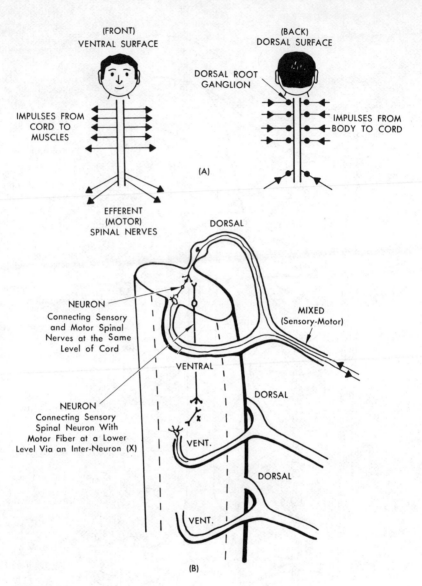

**FIGURE 3-5**

Spinal cord showing (A) afferent and efferent paths, and (B) autonomic components.

osition "to" or "toward" (*ad*)—describes this function of sensory neurons. See Figure 3-5.

In almost all cases, the pathway from receptor to sensory areas of the brain is interrupted frequently by synapses. The receptors trigger activity in a set of afferent neurons. These proceed toward the CNS for a distance and then terminate. Their axons make synaptic "connection" with the dendrites of the next set of afferents. These, in turn, go for some distance before terminating on yet another set of units. We say, then, that afferent transmission usually is *polysynaptic*. A convenient illustration of this is found in vision.[1] The receptors (rods and cones), by way of the bipolar cells, activate those (afferent) neurons whose axons form the optic nerve. Because, in the total chain of events, these are the first bona fide neurons, we call them *first-order* neurons. This bundle of fibers (the optic nerve) journeys back behind the eyes and then terminates in a structure called the *lateral geniculate nucleus* (LGN) of the *thalamus*. In fact, all sensory systems converge on the thalamus as a station on the way to other brain structures. They all terminate in different places within the thalamus, which contains a collection of cell bodies (nuclei) whose dendrites await this information coming from the sense organs. Any collection of cell bodies in the CNS is referred to as a *nucleus* (not to be confused with the nucleus of a single cell). Thus, the optic nerve fibers (axons) terminate on a *thalamic nucleus*. These cells, which receive the information carried by the first-order neurons of the optic nerve, are called, appropriately, second-order neurons. It should now be clear what is meant by "third-order," "fourth-order," . . . "$n^{th}$-order" neurons.

In most instances, although there are important exceptions, the destination of sensory messages in *man* is somewhere in the great cerebral mantle, somewhere within the cerebral hemispheres shown in Figure 3-3. Traditionally, it is here that the "machine's" enlightenment is presumed to occur. We will defer this question and examine first the "output" systems.

## ANATOMICAL FEATURES OF MOTOR SYSTEMS

In major respects, the response side of the nervous system is somewhat like a reversed version of the sensory side. The events of interest begin in the CNS (brain and spinal cord) and end in the PNS (peripheral nervous system). Since information is carried *away from* the CNS, the fibers are called *efferents* (the Latin *e* meaning "from"). Again, the pathways are usually polysynaptic; the first-order neurons are within the CNS, and the $n^{th}$-order units are in the PNS. (See Figure 3-6.)

In sensory systems, receptors are the first structures to be involved. In motor systems, the motor "endplates" are the last. They reside within the tissues of muscles and glands and, when activated,

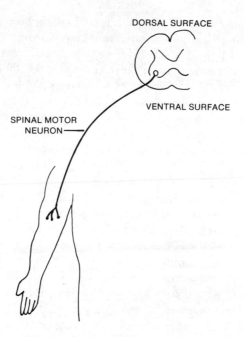

**FIGURE 3-6**
Major neural pathways are either monosynaptic or polysynaptic. This sketch illustrates a monosynaptic motor pathway from the ventral root of the spinal cord to the muscle fibers of the arm.

cause contractions. Muscular contractions give rise to movement of the body; glandular activation results in glandular secretions.

The last link in the polysynaptic chain that leads to movement was named very dramatically by the great neurophysiologist Sir Charles Sherrington *the final common path*. All events occurring before it are but preludes to action. (See Figure 3-7.)

## SENSORY-MOTOR CONNECTIONS

That structures participating in sensation and action have separate pathways to and from the CNS was first crudely demonstrated in 1810 by Sir Charles Bell and later, independently and with far greater precision, by François Magendie (1822). This principle of separate pathways is known as the *Bell-Magendie Law*.

Careful anatomical inspection of the spinal cord reveals *pairs* of nerves arranged symmetrically throughout its length. One member of

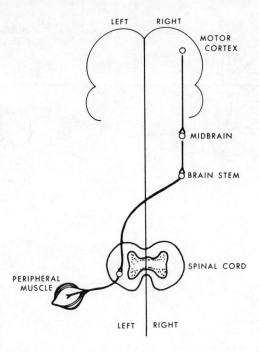

**FIGURE 3-7**

Sketch of motor pathway. Activity in right motor cortex travels down through (right) midbrain and (right) brainstem. At the level of the brainstem, the pathways cross to the left side and proceed down the left portion of the (ventral) cord. Efferent fiber exits from the ventral surface and invades striate muscle at the periphery.

the pair is attached to the front of the cord; the other member, to the back. When nerves on the front (*ventral*) surface are severed, paralysis ensues. The part of the body thus immobilized depends upon the level at which the surgical section is made. When nerves attached to the back (*dorsal*) surface are cut, movement is possible, but all sensation is lost. Again, the region thus desensitized depends upon the level at which the section is made. Through observations of this kind, Bell and Magendie demonstrated the independence of sensory and motor pathways. Afferent impulses enter the cord on the dorsal surface and are carried up to the brain. Motor signals originating in the brain travel down the cord and exit from the ventral surface to deliver their efferent commands to the muscles and glands.

In man, there are thirty-one pairs of spinal nerves. They are shown in Figure 3-8, together with some of the structures they serve. Eight of the pairs are called *cervical,* twelve *thoracic,* five *lumbar,* five

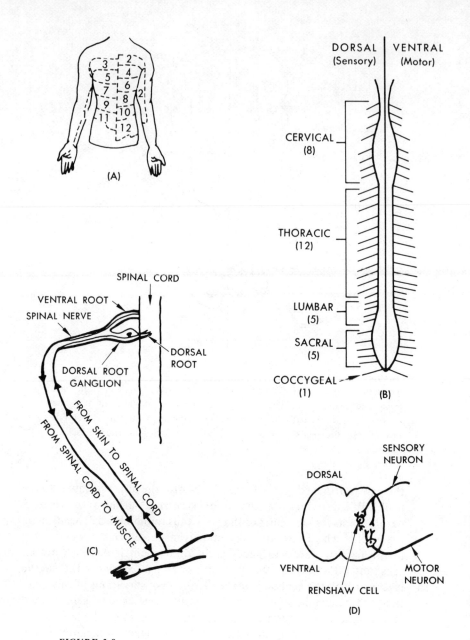

**FIGURE 3-8**

(A) Dermatomes of thoracic spinal nerves 2–12. (B) The 31 pairs of spinal nerves. (C) Separation of sensory (afferent) and motor (efferent) pathways. (D) Inhibition within the spinal cord. Impulses arriving from afferent neurons converge on the Renshaw cell as well as on motor neurons. The Renshaw cells inhibit the latter. This is the mechanism that participates in the "stretch" reflex; i.e., once muscle tissue is stretched (extended), inhibition is established so that further stretching is opposed while flexor muscles are engaged.

*sacral,* and one *coccygeal.* Each dorsal member of the pair reveals a swelling just before it enters the cord. The reason for this swelling is that at this point there is a cluster of cell bodies. As has been said, a collection of cell bodies in the CNS is called a nucleus. However, the cell bodies outside the cord are part of the PNS, and so a different term is used to distinguish them. In the peripheral nervous system, such a collection is called a *ganglion* (or, in plural form *ganglia*). And the bulge in the dorsal member of the pair of spinal nerves is called the *dorsal root ganglion.* In the ventral root, the cell bodies reside within the cord; therefore, no bulge appears.

Soon after leaving the cord (in the case of motor fibers) and just before entering the cord (in the case of sensory fibers), the efferent and afferent fibers run together; that is, the nerve is *mixed.* If it is sectioned at this point, both paralysis and insensitivity will result.

Both sensory and motor functions of a particular region of the body are mediated by the same level of the cord. The arm, for example, is served by spinal nerves at the levels of C-5 through C-8 (the fifth through the eighth cervical spinal nerves). We can actually "map" the body surface in terms of the spinal nerves that feed it. As Figure 3-8 shows, there is considerable overlap; that is, a given spinal pair serves a rather diffuse area. The areas themselves are called *dermatomes* (from *derma,* meaning "skin").

## GENERAL ORGANIZATION WITHIN THE CORD

Just as sensory and motor pathways in the PNS are polysynaptic, connections within the CNS also often involve multiple connections. A sensory neuron forming part of the dorsal root does not send its axon all the way to the thalamus or other brain regions. Instead, it may terminate as soon as it enters the cord, or it may proceed upward for a short distance and terminate there. Some such fibers, as soon as they get inside the cord, terminate and form synaptic connections with the dendrites and cell bodies of spinal *efferent* neurons (motor neurons). Through this arrangement, a sensory message can activate spinal motor nerves but never get to the brain. The entire transaction occurs within the cord, so that movement can be initiated by a sensory event in the absence of participation by the brain. Such transactions (shown in Figure 3–8) are called *spinal reflexes.* The decapitated frog will still withdraw his leg when pricked by a pin. The sequence is mediated entirely at a specific spinal level; that is, within a given segment of the cord. More complex connections, which allow *suprasegmental* reflexes where a sensory event at one level produces a motor response at a different level (segment), can also be demonstrated in the animal whose spinal cord has been severed from the brain. An example is the "scratch" reflex. If the animal's back is tickled—say, over the shoulder blade—the hind limb on the same side will be brought up to scratch the spot. In this case, sensory events at one level recruit motor reflexes from a lower segment. Still other reflexes involve stimulation on one side and the reflex responding of the other side. An example of this kind of organization is the crossed-extension reflex. The left hind limb of the animal is flexed and the right hind limb responds by extending downward. These various reflexes indicate that a surprising degree of behavioral complexity is possible to an animal with no more than a functioning spinal cord.

This concludes our general "map" of the system. At this point, we have at least a modest idea of the pathways involved in carrying the impulse. With the mechanism and map, we can begin the more interesting undertaking, the journey itself. If the materialists are to remain hopeful, we should be able to discover various psychological events taking place in different regions. At least we should find reliable neurophysiological correlates of these events.

## NOTES AND REFERENCES

1. The choice of vision is convenient but not representative. The retina evolves embryologically from the same primordium as the central nervous system and is not really a "sensory-peripheral" system. Yet its organization is so well studied that it serves as a proper illustration.

# 4
# Coming to Our Senses

Although neuropsychologists still do not presume to explain *how* human beings and animals see, hear, taste, etc., they have compiled an abundance of information about what happens neurophysiologically when seeing, hearing, or tasting occurs. How have these neural scientists secured this information? That is, what are the principal methods of the neural sciences? If we are to evaluate any conclusions properly, we must know how they were arrived at, what methods were used. Some methods require that we accept an answer "on faith." Others claim actually to demonstrate a relationship between events when really they have only demonstrated a relationship between words. For example, Bartholomew contended that we know of the existence of a "vital spirit" from our knowledge of the "soul." In actuality, he demonstrated the existence of neither.

A method in science is always based upon some prior assumption; hence, the dependence of science upon philosophy. A man makes a scale because he assumes that things have weight. But then something very subtle may occur. Now that he has the scale, his confidence in it may force him to conclude that anything without weight does not exist; hence, the dependence of philosophy upon science. Our assumptions generate methods, our methods lead to findings, our findings alter our assumptions, and on and on it goes.

### Clinical Observation

The caveman very probably acquired some understanding of clinical neurology. As a successful hunter, he would have had to learn not only the habits of his prey but also their vulnerabilities. He probably learned early that the effects of delivering blows to the body of an animal or an enemy depended upon where the blows were struck. Within his own community, he could well have discovered that blindness results from severe injuries to the back of the skull; paralyses, from spinal injuries; unconsciousness, from damage anywhere on the skull. By the time Egypt had developed medicine, there were even remedies for some of these conditions—although there is no evidence of a unifying theory to account for the success of the remedies.

By the seventeenth century, matters had progressed well beyond the accidents of the cave and the first-aid of Egypt. Physicians now actually recorded their clinical observations. As a result, by 1800 they had acquired considerable evidence that certain major brain structures are related to certain functions. During this same period, English philosophers were developing a system of thought known as *empiricism*. Recall from Chapter 1 that the empiricists held that the "contents of the mind" are determined solely by *experience;* accordingly, all that one knows or ever can know is acquired through the senses. In other words, in opposition to the idealist and nativist view, the empiricist rejects the notion of *innate* ideas independent of the senses.

A very important development in the empiricist movement was occurring in Scotland during the eighteenth century, a development called *faculty psychology*. According to the proponents of faculty psychology, each of the senses allows the development of a particular kind of knowledge; that is, certain distinguishable mental *faculties* are uniquely anchored to basic sensory processes. When the faculty psychology of the Scottish empiricists was added to the materialistic psychology of Germany and France, the result was unfortunate; for this first great synthesis of psychology and biology gave us *phrenology*. The father of the movement was a respected anatomist named Franz Joseph Gall; his missionary and agent was the psychologist G. Spurzheim. The development of phrenology grew from just a few fundamental assumptions: (1) that the mind is but the activity of the brain, (2) that the mind consists of separate faculties, (3) that each of the faculties is "housed" within specific structures of the brain, (4) that people differ in the endowment of these faculties because they differ in the amount of brain devoted to each of them, (5) that these differences are innate or are secondary to injury, (6) that the more of the brain involved in the control and expression of a particular faculty, the more cranial volume it will occupy, (7) that the prominence and importance of these brain areas can be determined by a careful palpation of the head. Thus, by feeling around for the assorted bumps and crannies of the skull surface, the physician is able to ascertain the basic personality and the behavioral capacities and predispositions of his patient. To assist them in this vital work, Gall and Spurzheim published *phrenology maps* like the one shown in Figure 4-1. There are, according to this scheme, some thirty-five faculties, only fourteen of them intellectual; The others are "af-

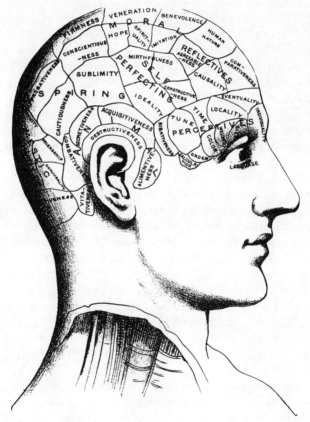

**FIGURE 4-1**
Phrenology head with regions of human capacities. (The Bettmann Archive.)

fective," running the gamut from the *desire to live* to such heady qualities as *marvelousness.* In his polemical six volumes Gall tirelessly insists that:

> I have established the fact by a great many proofs . . . that the brain alone has the great prerogative of being the organ of the mind. . . . The moral and intellectual dispositions are innate; their manifestation depends on organization; the brain is exclusively the organ of the mind; the brain is composed of as many particular and independent organs as there are fundamental powers of the mind; —these four incontestable principles form the basis of the whole physiology of the brain.

We don't have any phrenology journals anymore—the last one died in Philadelphia in 1911—although there may be a society or two still burdened by the name. Yet, at the height of Gall's fame (1830's), the movement could claim over seventeen periodicals, a wide and devout audience, and the praise of more than one authority.

Fortunately for the history of science, most of the truly outstanding specialists in neurology dismissed phrenology as poppycock. Among the leaders of the opposition was Pierre Flourens (1794–1867), whose clinical observations and research with animals clearly indicated far less specific localization of functions within the brain than phrenology required. For instance, as Flourens recognized, sometimes relatively large areas of the brain can suffer injury with only marginal deficits ensuing; in other instances, small regions of pathology can lead to profound disorders.

As diagnostic methods become more precise, it becomes possible to correlate very specific deficits with the destruction of various brain "centers." Some of these relationships will be taken up later. For now, we must recognize that the clinical method, even when bolstered by elegant instruments, has certain limitations. First, the clinician usually knows little about the patient's abilities prior to his illness or injury, so that he can only guess at the causes and severity of the patient's deficit. He can only *assume* that the patient was "normal" before his illness and that his deficits are the result of the particular problem that has been diagnosed. To discover, for example, that a tumor in area $X$ exists and that the patient has poor recall does not necessarily imply that the ability to recall depends upon $X$. The patient may well have always been poor in his ability to recall events. It is in the nature of the clinic that very little is known of a patient's abilities until illness degrades them.

Another limitation of the clinical method is that Nature is a clumsy surgeon. An injury or a disease almost never singles out some highly circumscribed area of the brain and affects only its functions.

Far more typically, the patient arrives with an assortment of problems: vascular diseases that implicate the entire CNS; tumors that are growing and invading adjacent regions; infections that swell and heat extensive masses of cerebral tissue; superficial and penetrating traumas that shock the entire cranial mass and produce injuries over widespread and seemingly independent locations. It is impossible to ascertain the relationship between structure $X$ and function $Y$ when structure $X$ is only one of many that have been disturbed.

Finally, before any relationships can be established, the variables to be related must be specified in an unambiguous, preferably quantitative, manner. The caveman recognized that an animal struck on the head fell in a heap. The only conclusion possible from this observation is that standing and the head are somehow related. With greater care, he could have systematically distributed his blows to different parts of the skull and carefully metered their force. The more meticulous caveman would then have had a better but still crude sense of the relationship between brain and behavior. To do any better, he would actually have to enter the head and control more or less precisely the location of his intrusions. The caveman did no such thing. In fact, no one did until the nineteenth century, when *ablative surgery* (from *ablation,* which means "removal" or "cutting away") was introduced.

### Ablative Surgery

Pierre Flourens, although not the first to explore the nervous system of animals surgically, was among the first to do so with great skill, commendable imagination, and theoretical acumen. Combining clinical surgery on man with experimental surgery on animals, Flourens contributed facts about the functional organization of the nervous system that have stood the test of a century. Much of what is still taught in high school about the medulla oblongata and the control of respiration, about the cerebellum and muscular coordination, about the cerebrum and "higher" functions, was first disclosed through the efforts of Flourens.

The ablation technique remains a common tool in studies of brain function. The assumptions behind it are straightforward: (1) psychological and biological functions are controlled by the brain; (2) if a given function is under the control of a particular structure, removal or destruction of that structure should lead to the elimination or degradation of that function.

However, the ablation technique suffers from many of the same limitations encountered in clinical assessments. Man may be a better surgeon than Nature, but he is far from perfect and the brain is awesomely interconnected. As a result, when the surgeon removes structure $X$, he cannot guarantee that he has disturbed nothing else. Thus, when he ablates $X$ and the animal fails to do $Y$, that does not prove that $X$ causes $Y$; for perhaps certain fibers that pass through $X$ are really necessary for $Y$, whereas $X$ is only incidentally involved. Then there is the problem of specifying the deficit. Suppose that $X$ is removed and nothing happens. Does that mean that $X$ is responsible for nothing, or simply that its function has not been found? There is the correlated problem of *recovery of function*. Many structures, when removed, leave the animal severely incapacitated. In time, however, the once-lost functions are restored. Since neurons in the CNS do not regenerate when destroyed,[1] structure $X$ has surely not been restored. But the ability *has*. What does this say about the role of $X$ initially? Finally, there is the "sampling" problem. On what basis do we select $X$ in the first place? There are ten to fifteen billion neurons in the head, and we have no hope of ablating them one at a time. Moreover, the CNS does not operate "one at a time." Thus, we must have some plan of action. But selecting one population of cells inevitably means ignoring others or at least delaying examination of them. Given the complexity of the brain, the combinatorial possibilities are inexhaustible.

It is still fashionable to chide Aristotle for having placed the mind in the heart. We should remember, however, how he reached this absurd conclusion. If the head of a chicken is cut off, he will continue to run around frantically; but if his heart is removed, all vital functions, all motion, all sensation cease. Here is an example of deductions drawn from ablative surgery. We may surmise that if Aristotle had been a better experimenter he would have discovered that spinal reflexes allow the headless bird to run for cover. But this criticism is inescapable when we limit ourselves to ablations. There is no end to the number of separate structures and combinations of structures that may be studied.

### Electrical Stimulation

Each method in neuropsychology and neurology is designed to compensate for the limitations implicit in alternatives. After the work of Galvani, Volta, and Helmholtz, scientists were in possession of two indispensable bits of knowledge: (1) that communication within the nervous system is electrical and (2) that this electrical activity can be both induced and recorded. One of the most important applications of these insights occurred in 1870 at the University of Berlin. There, two physiologists, Fritsch and Hitzig, removed the bony barrier to the brain of a dog and stimulated the cortex with a weak electrical signal. In a novel reversal of policy, they had already applied a galvanic current to the back of the head of a man and had elicited eye movements. Armed with this observation, they proceeded to explore the canine cortex directly. Sure enough, as they applied their weak shock to successively displaced areas of the "motor" cortex, the dog's paws, then lower extremities, then abdomen, then eyes responded with activity. The stronger the stimulus, the more general were the movements. With very weak currents, they were able to excite activity in small groups of muscles.

It is little more than a century since Fritsch and Hitzig reported their amazing results. In the years since, smaller electrodes, better amplifiers, and humane anesthetics (which, unforgivably, were not used in the earliest studies) have been developed. With *microelectrodes,* stimuli can be limited to one or just a few cells; at the same time, the activity that occurs in the area—when stimulated or when unstimulated—can be recorded. Other instruments control the placement of electrodes to within small fractions of a millimeter. With small enough electrodes, the damage resulting from insertion is marginal; consequently, an animal can live out a normal life carrying them around in his head. At desired times, experimenters can plug the animal into stimulators or recorders and see how things are going. This method of electrical stimulation and recording is the most sophisticated yet developed and has provided most of the information available about the relationship between brain activity on the one hand and psychological functions on the other.

Even electrical stimulation, however, has serious limitations. For one thing, there is the same relentless sampling problem. An electrode cannot be put into every cell. Then, too, there is the artificiality of it all. Neither man nor beast wanders through the world with electrodes in his head unless he has been captured by the army of science. Can we be sure, when we observe the consequences of stimulation, that we are looking at a version of the normal sequence of events? That event $Y$ *can* be produced by stimulating structure $X$ does not prove that, under ordinary circumstances, the activity of $X$ gives rise to $Y$. There is also the more basic difficulty of species differences. That $X$ gives rise to $Y$ in the salamander or even the monkey does not necessarily indicate that the same relationship will hold when we examine man. This, of course, is a problem in *all* animal research. In some instances, it need not be taken too seriously. That is, we have warranted confidence that processes such as sugar metabolism, the circulation of blood, and the salivary reflex unfold in similar fashion among all the higher species. But, with man, the psychological attributes of greatest complexity (language, thought, feeling, etc.) are so exceptional—or seem to be so exceptional—that the basic biological processes may also be unique.[2]

### Chemical Analyses

In a fundamental respect, the nervous system is just an elaborate means by which chemical events can be produced over great distances and with great speed. As we saw in Chapter 2, the nervous impulse has the special ability to induce synaptic events that are chemical in nature. By its nature, the impulse is too short-lived to account for the persistence of effects in our minds. Thus, once we look for long-term mechanisms, it is natural for the search to begin with chemical processes. This search is among the most recent. The assumptions behind it, in addition to what has just been said, are these: The basic processes of biological systems are biochemical. Experience comes to have profound effects upon us. These effects, if they are to persist, must be stored. If the biochemistry of organisms is examined both before and after some experimental treatment, specific chemical alterations should be found. But, again, only a small fraction of all the chemicals in the body can be isolated in any one experiment. Moreover, the treatments used to change the "experience" of the animal are, per force, arbitrary. When later we examine "memory molecules" and the like, more will be said on this problem.

### Gross Recordings

Neural scientists also make use of instruments that measure the general activity of the nervous system. The most widely used of such instruments is the electroencephalograph (EEG), which records the intrinsic and rhythmic activity of the living brain. This activity was noted in animals and recorded from the skull surface by Catton as early as 1875. Not until the pioneering studies of Hans Berger, however, was human brain activity noted and made recordable. Berger published his findings in 1929, many years after he made them—fearing rejection by his colleagues. Among other observations, he noted that the brain of a conscious, awake man, relaxed and with his eyes closed, waxes and wanes in its electrical discharges at a frequency between eight and twelve times per second. He called this activity the *alpha rhythm*. The alpha rhythm, as Berger demonstrated, is altered (a) when the subject performs mental calculations, (b) when visual and auditory stimuli are presented, (c) when the subject is aroused or otherwise made to become alert, (d) when the subject is asleep. (See Figure 4-2.) Later investigators added

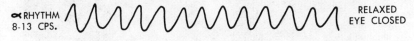

α RHYTHM
8-13 CPS.

RELAXED
EYE CLOSED

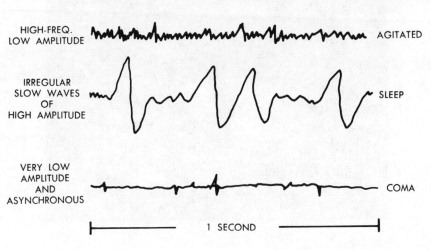

HIGH-FREQ.
LOW AMPLITUDE

AGITATED

IRREGULAR
SLOW WAVES
OF
HIGH AMPLITUDE

SLEEP

VERY LOW
AMPLITUDE
AND
ASYNCHRONOUS

COMA

1 SECOND

**FIGURE 4-2**
EEG recordings (schematic).

considerably to Berger's early experiments, so that the EEG is now used to monitor sleep, to detect certain neurological problems (epilepsy, encephalitis, certain types of tumor), and as an index of alertness. These, however, are but correlates.[3] That is, neural scientists now know that the EEG looks a certain way when a subject sleeps and a very different way when he is aroused, but they do not know *why* this is so. They can only speculate.

A second type of gross recording involves not the intrinsic activity of the brain but the *evoked* activity. When a stimulus is delivered to a sense organ, the resulting neural activity alters the electrical events in the brain. Recorded through the scalp and skull, such alterations are of extremely low amplitude. Whereas the EEG alpha rhythm may be of the order of 50–100 microvolts (millionths of a volt), the *evoked response* may only be a few microvolts. Therefore, the evoked signal is buried in the larger EEG signal. However, computers can be programmed to "add up" a number of these small signals, more or less canceling out the background activity, and obtain what is called an *averaged evoked response* (See Figure 4–3). With it, the response of large populations of cortical cells to a variety of stimuli can be assessed.[4]

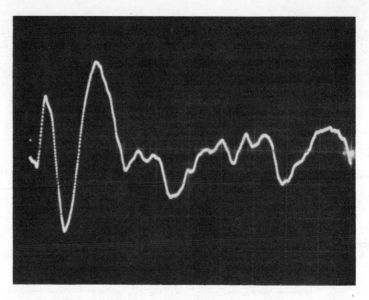

**FIGURE 4-3**
Visual averaged evoked response obtained from average of 50 presentations of light flash. Baseline = 800 msec. Note major component between 100 and 200 msec.

## NEURAL CORRELATES OF SENSATION AND PERCEPTION

Each of the foregoing methods has been employed in a variety of contexts and at various levels of neural organization. There is no need to catalog everything that has been discovered in order to get the gist of what the neural sciences are in a position to tell us. In fact, we need not examine every sense. Current findings indicate that the same general principles operate in all sensory systems, so that a demonstration of what is taking place in some of them will be enough to suggest what is probably taking place in all of them. And, to keep things as uncluttered as possible, we can limit our examination to rather broad categories, such as the quantity and quality of certain sensations. We begin with vision, about which we know the most, and ask as fundamental a question as is possible: *How do I know that light is present?* Alas, this is not fundamental. It is profound, for the verb "know" implies complexities quite separate from the mere act of sight. Let us try to make the question less quarrelsome. *What neural events are reliably correlated with my report of the presence of light?*

### Brightness

When light strikes the retina, the decomposition of pigments in the rods and cones results in an electrical event known as the *early receptor potential*. Only after this event has occurred can we find impulse activity in the optic nerve—aside from that background activity that occurs in nerves all the time. The early receptor potential is just one of a number of nonimpulsive electrical events taking place in the retina. Later graded signals can be recorded from the bipolar cells as well as from the amacrine and horizontal layers sketched in the previous chapter.

The connections among units forming the retina are complex and prodigious. Even the lowly crab (*Limulus*) has generous interrelations. The crab is an especially good animal for visual studies because the chain from receptors to optic nerve fibers, unlike that of the primate, is relatively simple and can quite easily be broken. The eye of the crab, like that of all arthropods, is *compound;* that is, made up of a number of smaller "eyes" distributed over the entire surface. Each individual eye is called an *ommatidium* (See Figure 4-4), consisting of a lens that focuses light on a little pool of pigment. When the pigment is bleached, an electrical potential is generated; when this potential reaches some critical value, impulses occur in the small fiber extending from the ommatidium. Thus, this simple unit "codes" the light; that is, the way that impulses are initiated depends upon the physical properties of the light. One of the first measurements ever

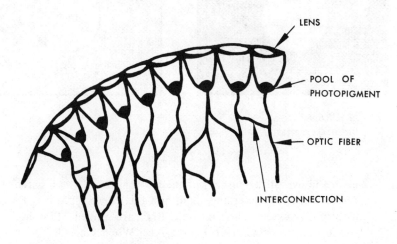

**FIGURE 4-4**
Schematic drawing of Limulus compound eye.

made on this preparation disclosed a very precise relationship between light intensity and the "firing" rate of the fiber. In fact, the number of impulses initiated in one second increases linearly with each logarithmic increase in the intensity of the stimulus. The relationship is described by the equation $R = k \log_{10} S$ where $R$ is the response of the fiber (expressed in impulses per second); $S$ is the stimulus intensity; and $k$ is a constant that depends, among other things, on the temperature of the preparation, how long it has been responding, and the particular unit from which the measures are taken.

The same relationship is found in *human* vision. It is known as *Fechner's Law*, and is indifferent to the species of animal whose visual functions it describes.

### Contrast

Gray paper against a black background looks much brighter than the same paper against a background that is only slightly grayer (see Figure 4–5). The apparent brightness of a stimulus seems to depend

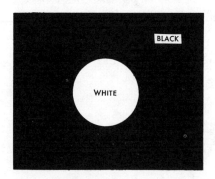 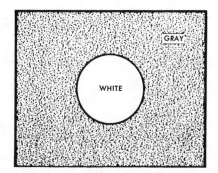

**FIGURE 4-5**
Brightness contrast.

upon the overall brightness of the field in which it is located. Little *Limulus* tells us something about how this effect is produced. Even in its primitive eye, neighboring ommatidia are connected by short interconnecting processes (see Figure 4–6). When Unit *A* is stimulated, the recorded impulses in its fiber will look something like this: ⊥⊥⊥⊥⊥⊥⊥⊥⊥⊥⊥ . If, however, neighboring unit *B* is stimulated while *A* is still responding, activity in *A* is reduced, or *inhibited*. As

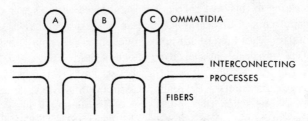

FIGURE 4-6

the impulse rate in *B* is increased, the concurrent activity in *A* is inhibited proportionately. If unit *C* (which, although connected to *B*, has no connections with *A*) is stimulated while both *A* and *B* are responding, the activity in *B* is now inhibited and the effect of this is to *disinhibit* unit *A*.

In human vision, the processes of inhibition and disinhibition are far more complex, since the interconnections among retinal rods and cones are much more extensive. These processes are essential if we are to enjoy sharp images. The lens of the human eye is imperfect, and the light admitted by it must travel through the fluids of the eye and through layers of cells before reaching the rods and cones. Thus, a point of light outside the eye will come to be represented as a blur of light on the retina. This *optically* blurry image is converted into an *electrically* clear image by the process of *lateral inhibition*. Neighboring units form a circle of mutually inhibiting activity such that the centrally stimulated cells can come to dominate the experience. Thus, while a rather broad blur is cast across the retina, only the more intensely stimulated units send messages along the optic nerve and to the brain.

### Color and Acuity

Color is a sensible *quality* not something implicit in the stimulus as intensity (quantity) is. Since our nerves "code" intensity by varying their impulse rates, a different mechanism is necessary for the coding of color; otherwise, we would not be able to distinguish between changes in brightness and changes in the wavelength (color) of light. As it happens, however, the two codes—the one for intensity and the one for wavelength—do depend in part on a common mechanism, and that is why the apparent color of a stimulus may change as its brightness changes. But there is also a separation of mechanisms for the two sensations, and it is based upon what Johannes Müller (Helmholtz's teacher) called the *Law of Specific Nerve Energies*. According to this law, each nerve is endowed with a specific potential for experience. For example, once an optic nerve fiber is stimulated, no matter what kind of stimulus (mechanical, thermal, electrical, etc.) is used, the resulting sensation is one of light. That is, *the experience is not in the stimulus; it is in the nerves.* This law is a biological example of certain tenets prevailing in German philosophy, since Müller lived at a time when the philosophy of Immanuel Kant dominated European thought. We will meet with Kant again in the last chapter. For present purposes, we note only that Kant's theory of knowledge is *nativistic* and *idealistic.* He reasoned that fundamental aspects of human knowledge do not derive from experience but are based, instead, upon inborn dispositions of the mind. In fact, were it not for these innate (*a priori*) characteristics, our experiences would have neither meaning nor organization. Müller's Law of Specific Nerve Energies supported the Kantian contention that the nature of experience is determined by the native endowments of the perceiver.

What gives a nerve its specific energy is not something about the nerve itself. A sensory fiber in the optic nerve looks much like a fiber in the auditory nerve or, for that matter, like one in the nose. Moreover, impulses in one sensory system are of the same form as those traveling in other sensory systems. The telling difference is their destination. That is, the final determinant of experience is the location within the central nervous system toward which the sensory messages are directed. Thus, two factors are always involved in giving rise to a particular sensory event. The first is the coding that takes place in the sensory nerves. The "code" is in terms of both impulse rate and the particular nerve that is excited. The second factor is the particular region of the brain that receives this coded information. In vision, the relationship between a given place on the retina and a given place in the "visual brain" is so precise, so geometrically elegant, that even a sketch of it has the quality of a painting. (See Figure 4-7.)

First, the fibers—about a million of them in man—travel back from the retina into the brain as optic nerves. Keep in mind that the information impinging on about 130,000,000 rods and cones had been *transformed,* by inhibition and disinhibition, and *reduced* in that the ratio of receptors (rods and cones) to fibers is about 130:1. This reduction takes place when large pools of receptors converge on but a few bipolar cells and these, in turn, feed into even fewer ganglion cells. (The axons of these ganglion cells are the fibers of the optic nerve.) In the most central region of the retina, the *fovea,* there are only cones. Here, each cone has its own bipolar cell,[5] and each bipolar cell feeds but one ganglion cell. Thus, in foveal vision anything that strikes adjacent cells has a good chance of being processed by two optic nerve

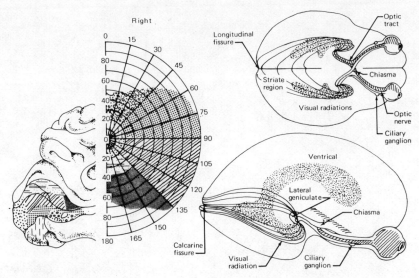

**FIGURE 4-7**

Visual pathways from retina to visual cortex. Note the point-to-point projection of fibers from specific retinal areas to specific cortical regions. (Top and middle figures adapted from J. C. Fox and W. J. German [1936], Macular Vision Following Cerebral Resection. *Archives of Neurology and Psychiatry, 35,* 808–826; bottom figure from G. Holmes [1945], The Organization of the Visual Cortex in Man. *Proceedings of the Royal Society* [London], *132B,* 348–361.)

fibers. Foveal vision thus allows incredibly great *acuity*. Suppose, for example, that two narrow stripes are presented to the eye, with the distance between the stripes equivalent to the separation between two adjacent cones within the fovea. Since each cone will be able to represent its stimulus in a separate fiber of the optic nerve, the eye can discern that indeed two stripes, rather than one thick one, are "out there." Away from the center of the retina more and more rods appear until at the extreme periphery, there are *only* rods. They are much more plentiful and they pool their resources. (See Figure 4-8.) For example, several hundred rods may converge on perhaps twenty or thirty bipolar cells, and these in turn may terminate on, say, five or ten ganglion cells. Thus, when several hundred rods have their activity represented, finally, in only five fibers in the optic nerve (a 60:1 reduction in what we may call information channels), poor visual acuity results. Since the two stripes now fall on receptors that ulti- mately feed the same fiber in the optic nerve, there is no code for "twoness" at the periphery of the retina. Instead, the stripes are simply added and one thick stripe discerned. But herein resides the

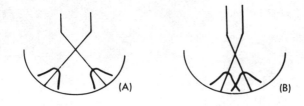

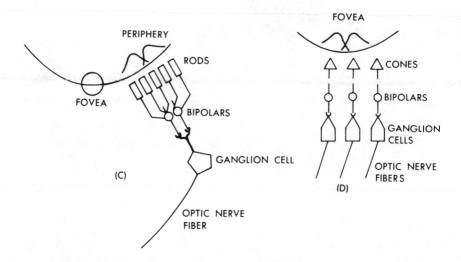

**FIGURE 4-8**

Information processing in the retina. (A) Wide separation of retinal stimuli allows perception of two strips. (B) Overlapping may lead to two appearing as only one. (C) Poor acuity due to pooling of rod responses. (D) Excellent acuity because of separate cone pathways.

great sensitivity of peripheral vision in the matter of *brightness*. A stimulus that is too weak to excite a foveal cone will not be seen even if it is delivered to many foveal cones, because each of their associated optic nerve fibers remains "untriggered." At the periphery, however, each rod can add its *subthreshold* response to a larger pool; by this *spatial summation* of intensities, the stimulus that is too dim to see when it is looked at head on becomes visible out of "the corner of the eye."

The information carried in optic nerve fibers associated with rods does not allow us to judge the color of a stimulus. For this reason, we call rod function *achromatic*. Although rods do contain photopigments, which are "bleached" differently by lights of different wavelengths, the experience of color is not possible at the end of this process. Throughout the entire animal kingdom, color vision is *cone* vision. Thus, any animal whose retina is devoid of cones will necessarily be a color-blind animal.

In most animals with cone vision, the cones contain not one but at least three different kinds of photopigment. And, if the goldfish retina is representative, there are at least three types of cone, each with a unique photopigment. One of these pigments is decomposed most quickly in the presence of short-wavelength (for instance, blue) light. Another pigment absorbs most efficiently in a middle region (for instance, green-yellow). A third pigment has its maximum absorption of light at the long-wavelength end of the spectrum (red). Light from almost anywhere on the visible spectrum will bleach some of the cone pigment; however, a particular region of the spectrum will have a maximum effect, depending upon the particular pigment in the cone. (See Figure 4-9.) Once the bleaching proceeds to a certain point, the receptor potential develops and excites the bipolar cell. At this point, a very original kind of color coding takes place. As we have seen, the resting potential of cells is $-70$ mv; an increase in this value (for example, to $-80$ mv or $-90$ mv) is *hyperpolarization,* while a decrease is *hypopolarization.* In the cells beyond the receptors, either of these events will occur depending upon the wavelength (color) of the light stimulating the receptor. We call these cells either "blue-yellow+" (hyperpolarizing in the presence of blue light, depolarizing in the presence of yellow) or "yellow- blue+" or "red+ green-" or "green+ red-." All four types exist. A cell excited by red will be inhibited by green and vice versa. A cell excited by blue will be inhibited by yellow and vice versa. And the coded impulses in the optic nerve are determined by the positive or negative responses of these units. A similar mechanism is found at the first way-station of the optic pathway, the thalamus. Here, in the *lateral geniculate nucleus* (LGN) the fibers of the optic nerve terminate. These fibers make synaptic connections with neurons that are, like most neurons in the nervous system, always active. And in the cells of the LGN we find the same antagonistic or *opponent process* as in the retina. That is, the impulses per second in an LGN unit will either increase or decrease, depending on the color of the light delivered to the eyes of the animal.

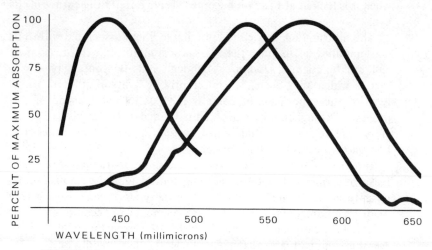

**FIGURE 4-9**

Spectral absorption by photopigments in the retinal cones of the monkey. Three distinct "peaks" are apparent; one in the blue region of the spectrum, one in the green, and one in the red. Observe the considerable overlap in the photochemical reactions of the three types of cones. (Based upon the data of E. F. MacNichol [1964]. Three-pigment Color Vision. *Scientific American, 211,* 48–56.)

Again, there are two pairs of opponent processes: blue+ yellow−, blue− yellow+, green+ red−, and green− red+. In this way, both the rate of impulses and the particular units involved serve as the codes for the experience of color. From the LGN, fibers proceed back to the *visual cortex;* here, too, there seem to be special cells that respond one way to one range of wavelengths and an opposite way to the complementary range. (See Figure 4-10.)

### Form Perception

Kant asserted that there is knowledge prior to experience, that it is native to the mind, and that it was by these native endowments that the effects of stimulation were determined.

Can we decide on the merits of this allegation by examining the retina of the frog? I think not. However, there is at least the intimation of "native ideas" when we observe the nearly miraculous equipment of the frog retina—equipment that detects bugs, senses motion, waits for changes in brightness.

Using microelectrodes, investigators have examined the electrical responses of different retinal cells in the retina of the frog in the presence of a variety of stimuli. Some units "fire" only when a convex

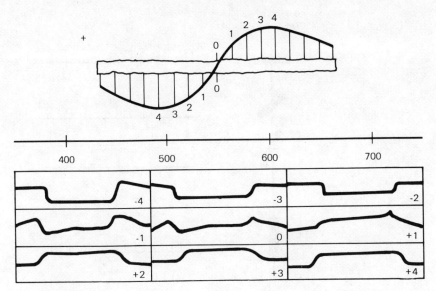

**FIGURE 4-10**

Opponent-processes in the retina of the fish. The top trace shows the amplitude
of electrical changes resulting from stimuli of different wavelengths. Changes
have negative polarity in the region between 400 and 500 millimicrons; changes
have positive polarity in the region from 600 to 700. In the boxes below, the
actual changes in polarity corresponding to 0, +1, +2, +3, and +4 and 0, −1,
−2, −3, and −4 are shown. Because of its shape, the top trace has been called
the S-potential. (Based upon the data of E. F. MacNichol and G. Svaetichin
[1958], Electric Responses from Isolated Retinas of Fishes. *American Journal of
Ophthalmology, 46,* 26–40.)

shape is moved across the eye. Others respond to brightness changes
but are indifferent to shape. Others show a preference for certain an-
gles of orientation. In the more sophisticated cat, units of this kind are
located within the LGN and the neurons of the visual cortex. Just as
there is great "funneling" of information going from receptors to
optic nerve fibers (the 130:1 reduction mentioned earlier), there is an
inverse funneling at the other end. That is, by the time the optic nerve
fibers have impinged upon the LGN and the pathways from the LGN
arrive at the cortex, the number of cortical cells involved has
increased to hundreds of millions. In this way, a given cortical neuron
can be excited when any one of a larger number of cells on the retina
is stimulated. (See Figure 4-11.) Because such cortical neurons are receptive to stimulation from a relatively broad retinal field, they are

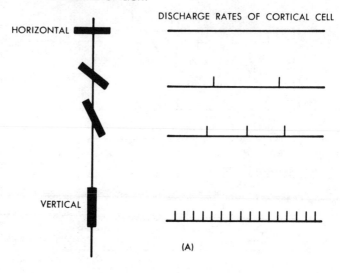

ORIENTATION OF
RECTANGLE OF LIGHT

HORIZONTAL

VERTICAL

DISCHARGE RATES OF CORTICAL CELL

(A)

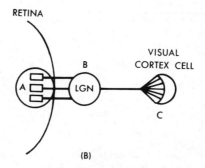

RETINA

B

VISUAL
CORTEX CELL

A    LGN

C

(B)

***FIGURE 4-11***

(A) Certain cells fire when stimuli fall on a given field of the retina. These are "on-center" units. Other cells are "off-center"; i.e., they are silenced by stimuli falling on the center of the retinal field. (B) Stimulus falling anywhere in field A of the retina will activate cell C in the visual cortex. Thus, A is said to be the *receptive field* of C.

called *cortical receptive fields*. The neuron will respond when stimulation enters its receptive field. How it responds depends upon the shape, brightness, velocity, and even color of the visual stimulus.

## OVERVIEW OF SENSORY CODES[6]

Each sense has its nuances, but each, too, operates according to general principles found everywhere in the nervous system. In audition, for example, the firing rate of fibers in the auditory nerve increases with the $\log_{10}$ of acoustic intensity. Pitch, a quality similar in hearing to what color is in vision, is coded in terms of both impulse rate and the specific units within first the basilar membrane and then the auditory nerve. Different pitches terminate on different regions of the major auditory pathways as well as on overlapping but differentiable regions of the auditory cortex. Different receptors seem to mediate the different skin sensations; touch, temperature (warm and cold), and pain. These receptors feed fibers with unique pathways within the spinal cord and with (probably) unique destinations in the thalamus. Here, too, intensity is coded by impulse *rate* while *quality* conforms more or less to the *Law of Specific Nerve Energies* or its more modern version which places the experience in the brain.

All this is to say that, as a detector and discriminator, the "machine" is exotic, but its general operating characteristics are well understood and its more basic features may well also surrender in the face of continued research.

### But How Do I Know?

Even Bartholomew, that poor unenlightened medievalist, had little difficulty accepting a mechanistic explanation of action and experience. Few would doubt it. Since we do see, hear, taste, etc., there must be some mechanism by which these functions are accomplished. But *vision* is not a neural impulse. After all, we can remove the optic nerve, drop it into an appropriate solution, stick it with a pin, and thereby generate impulses in it. *Is this vision?* Does the nerve *see?* Does the film in a camera, decomposing as it does when struck by light, *see* the landscape? For that matter, does a cat *see* a tree? We know only the contents of our minds and those of no other. To ask how Beethoven wrote such monumental music and to be told "with pen and paper" is not to be answered fully or even relevantly. To ask how we come to appreciate the genius of Monet and to be told about the early receptor potential and opponent processes in LGN is either to be cheated or chided. To comprehend the nature of our experiences demands more than a description of the mechanics of sensation. And, the neural sciences can offer more. To sensation must be added learning, memory, attention, emotion. In these processes one hopes to discover the missing elements.

Before turning to the neuropsychology of learning and memory, we should underscore the *relativistic* nature of research and theory in the area of sensory processes. It is important to recognize that the limitations in these areas are not only philosophical. They are semantic, conceptual, and procedural as well.

## THE RELATIVITY OF EXPERIENCE

Those who confront the data we've just examined frequently wonder what the difference is between *physiology* (which everyone knows about) and *physiological psychology* (a term which, to the novice, sounds forbidding and even rather "new-speak"). Often, there may be little immediate difference between the fields. But ultimately, the physiologist's goal is one of understanding biological processes per se, whereas the neuropsychologist's interest in the processes is only indirect. He is concerned ultimately with *psychological* phenomena, and his efforts in physiology are directed at concerns that manifest themselves in non-biological form. Thus, the physiologist may strive to make known the effects of stimulus intensity upon the firing rate of neurons. Having measured the relationship, he need refer to no other issue. The neuropsychologist taking measurements from the same neurons can not be sure of the *psychological* significance of the relationship until he examines his findings in the context of sensory *experience*. We can distinguish further by taking an example from vision. Suppose we record activity in the optic nerve of the cat in response to flashes of light delivered to the eye. We discover that each increase in the intensity of the flash is correlated with an increase in the firing rate recorded from the nerve. When we plot impulses per second against stimulus intensity, we obtain a logarithmically increasing function; i.e., $R = k \log_{10} (S)$, which is Fechner's Law. As indicated earlier, the neuropsychologist is intrigued by this result because the relationship between intensity and neural activity turns out to be the same as the psychophysical relationship between intensity and perceived brightness. That is, he derives some confidence in the psychophysical relationship by discovering a neural correlate of it. But had the neural relationship been very different—say, for example, that impuses per second did not change at all at any level of intensity—the neuropsychologist would quickly lose interest in this particular measure. Since his ultimate concern is the psychological fact of visual experience (in this case, the experience of brightness), he has no interest in any biological process that is entirely indifferent to the intensity of light. The physiologist, on the other hand, is concerned principally with the neural event. His interest in it *may* but *need not* be justified on the basis of psychological considerations.

This is a prologue to an important issue in neuropsychology. Since the physiological psychologist begins with the psychological fact and proceeds to search for its physiological precursors, his theories of neural function will be inescapably bound to his definitions and measurements of psychological processes. To take a trivial case, let us assume that a particular psychologist defines "happiness" in a dog as tail-wagging. That is, he assumes some internal state (happiness) on the basis of some behavioral measure (tail-wagging). Now he uses a physiological technique to determine which anatomical structures are involved in "happiness." The method he chooses is that of ablative surgery, and the first structure to be ablated is the tail. Conclusion: Tailless dogs are not capable of happiness. Of course, no conscientious or even conscious scientist would commit this particular folly. Yet there are very subtle contexts in which the same kind of absurdity is possible. We will explore these later. For now, we must recognize that all findings and theories in neuropsychology are based upon definitions of psychological events. Therefore, to assess the cogency of the neuropsychological proposition, we must examine the reasoning that underlies the definitions. We may profit from an examination of two sensory phenomena in which the *neuro* and the *psycho* features can create certain tensions. The first is the concept of a *threshold;* the second is that of *perfect pitch.*

### What is a Sensory Threshold?

Until a little more than a decade ago, the psychological definition of a sensory threshold went something like this: The absolute threshold is the smallest amount of stimulus energy necessary for the experimental subject to report the presence of the stimulus on 50 percent of the presentations. Actual experiments were designed to control the subject's guessing, to get the subject to report the presence of a stimulus only when he was certain that, indeed, it had been presented. Frequent "catch" trials were employed in which the subject was asked if the stimulus had been presented when, in fact, nothing had been. Reliable measurements were obtained—reliable in the sense that, on repeated tests, subjects tended to hit the 50 percent point at very nearly the same values of stimulus energy. However, when these psychophysical data were compared with neurophysiological findings, the nervous system proved far more sensitive than its owner. It was far easier (i.e., it took far less stimulus strength) to get a response from, say, a nerve in the arm than it took to get the subject up to the 50 percent detection level. Conclusion: The conscious, complex human being is so easily distracted, so difficult to control, and so inattentive that he simply cannot report stimuli to which his nervous system is reliably responding.

The foregoing conclusion, however, takes too much for granted. Traditional psychophysical procedures, in emphasizing the need *not to guess,* had actually built into the subject a high-threshold criterion. In other words, the subject is *not* easily distracted, *far* from difficult to control, and *very* attentive. Told not to guess under any circumstances, he adopts a criterion of responding that obscures the limits of his sensitivity. Suppose we employ a different procedure. The subject is told that each second during a stimulus trial a tone will sound gently in his earphones. Each tone marks one of five separate trial intervals. At some point during these five seconds, a dim light flash will be presented. His task, after the five seconds have elapsed, is to report the interval during which he thinks the flash was presented. In the event that he is wrong, he is then to "guess" in what other interval it may have occurred. He does this successively until he has, in effect, ranked the five intervals in terms of the probability that one of them contained the flash. Now, on his first guess, he has one chance in five of being right. That is, the *a priori* probability of a correct guess is 0.20. On his second guess, he has one chance in four ($p = 0.25$); on his third, one chance in three ($p = 0.33$); then one in two (0.50), and then one in one (1.0). When the threshold study is conducted in this manner, the subject "guesses" reliably better than chance would allow, even down to his fourth "guess." Furthermore, his threshold (considered in terms of the least energy at which his guesses are still above chance levels) is as low as what would be predicted from physiological values. In other words, when procedures that call forth high-threshold behavior are eliminated, the conscious, intact human subject can perform as if he were a nerve fiber.[7]

From the foregoing, we quickly appreciate the arbitrariness of any definition of a sensory threshold that does not take into account learning, motivation, instructions, and other variables that, in themselves, are nonsensory but that can have pronounced effects upon our measures of sensory capacity.

### Perfect Pitch

Some people show a remarkable ability to hum certain notes without the aid of any musical instrument. Moreover, if a note is played on a piano or violin, they can identify it with perfect accuracy. Such people are said to have *perfect pitch*. Now, the excitement and interest in this ability goes well beyond its capacity to enliven a cocktail party. From a physiological perspective, it would seem to be an absolutely Herculean feat for the nervous system to enjoy such perfection. Therefore, we would like to determine (a) whether it exists and (b) if it does, how it does. In regard to the first question, our answer alas will depend upon how we define this attribute and how we go about measuring it. If we impute "perfect" pitch to anyone who, at a distance, can recognize each note when it is struck on the piano, we are attributing perfection to an individual who has learned simply to identify 88 different sounds with 88 different names. Yet almost anyone can tell which of 88 different acquaintances he is speaking to over the telephone. And, in this case, the complexities of the acoustic signals are far greater than those emanating from a keyboard. Presumably, we would want to define "perfect pitch" in such a way as to eliminate or control the effects of practice and learning. That is, if we wish to impute perfection to a *sensory* process, we would want our definitions and our methods of measurement to isolate the sensory aspects of the tests, independent of cultural or experiential factors. In the instance of perfect pitch, we have an engineering model that we may use as a reference. Suppose we were told that a particular device (not a person) has perfect pitch. Now, "pitch" is a subjective experience, so we would want to substitute for it the term *frequency*. Thus, the attribute "perfect frequency discrimination" is something this device is purported to have. What this would imply is the following:

1. The device will respond differently to each change in frequency over the full range of its frequency sensitivity. Arbitrarily let's say the device was designed to receive and analyze sounds in the range from 100 to 1,000 cps. We should be able to get 901 different responses from this device, each one reliably associated with each possible frequency falling within its range of sensitivity.

2. No matter what we do to the distribution of acoustic energy, the device will faithfully report the separate frequencies present in any complex tone. For example, if we present three units of tone $A$, five units of tone $B$, and nine units of tone $C$, the device will report that all three were present and in what amounts. That is, it will be able to resolve the separate frequency components and assign magnitudes to each. It will, to use the technical term, perform a spectrum analysis on the input. It will thereby be able to report the amount of energy present in each component frequency.

3. Because of (2), it should not be possible to "fool" the device by

tampering with the intensity of certain harmonics. If we sound a note on the piano—say, middle $C$, which is a tone of 256 cps—not only is the pure tone (256) generated but also higher frequency "harmonics" of it (512 cps, 1,024 cps, etc.). However, each higher-order harmonic occurs with systematically diminishing intensity. Thus, the highest intensity is at 256 and the lowest, in our example, is at 1,024. Now, any device that serves as a "harmonic analyzer" must appreciate these relationships. Therefore, if we fed into it tones of 256, 512, and 1,024—*all at the same intensity*—it would distinguish between this collection of tones and the sound produced by striking middle $C$ and obtaining it and its harmonics. In other words, if we tampered with the intensity of any of the harmonics, the analyzer would immediately recognize that a pure tone had not been presented.

Given these criteria, we may wish to define "perfect pitch" more rigorously:

> An individual with "perfect pitch" is able to perform spectral (harmonic) analyses on complex inputs. One consequence of such analyses is that any alteration in the ratio of intensities among the fundamental and its harmonics will be recognized.

With this definition, our test for "perfect pitch" becomes more complicated than sounding notes on the piano. Instead, we present complex tones (two to $n$ separate frequencies) where we can control separately the intensity of each component. The listener must distinguish between those complex tones having different spectra. We may, for example, add $n$ units of 1,026 cps, subtract an equivalent amount at 1,024 cps, but keep the overall acoustic power constant. When these changes have been made in a complex input involving, as fundamentals, tones of 256, 513, and 1,024, can our listener detect them?

The foregoing experiments have not been performed, and at this time "perfect pitch" seems to be more of a compliment than a demonstrated ability. What is important for us to realize is that the neural mechanisms we search for are restricted to those permitted in our definitions of the psychological processes. If "perfect pitch" is the ability to recognize all 88 notes of the piano, we merely must find a neural code capable of distinguishing 88 different frequencies. If "perfect pitch" implies the ability to name not only the 88 notes but *combinations* of the 88, then we must look for a more complex code. And, finally, if by "perfect pitch" we mean the ability to perform harmonic analyses, then we must look for yet another variety of code. It should be clear, then, that a vicious but often unavoidable circle prods our ingenuity and arrests our progress in studying the neuropsychology of experience. Since our definitions of the experiences are relative, the mechanisms, even when isolated, are only a portion of the possible mechanisms.

## NOTES AND REFERENCES

1. This is not entirely correct. We do know that there is some "sprouting" of new neuronal tissue following destruction. However, the rate of regrowth is so agonizingly slow that, with respect to recovery of function, it might just as well be assumed that no regrowth has occurred at all. For a description of the methods used to study neuronal regeneration in the CNS, see J. E. Rose, L. I. Malis, and C. P. Baker, *Sensory Communication*, W. Rosenblith (Ed.), (Cambridge: M.I.T. Press, 1961), pp. 279–301.

2. This point is worth amplifying. We gain confidence in neuropsychology from the fact that there is good comparability between, for example, the pigment photochemistry of the monkey and that of man or between fat metabolism in the two species. The justification of this confidence is diluted, however, when we confront processes that are not shared or not equivalently shared by two species. Linguistic processes, for example, are either man's exclusively or, if found elsewhere in phylogeny, are so different in nonhumans that a comparative approach is impossible. For example, if man is the only animal with language (as language is defined in the last chapter) and if, by virtue of this capacity, human learning, perception, and emotion are unique, then a good deal of what we have learned about the neurophysiology of learning, emotion, and perception in animal research will be of questionable generalizability.

3. EEG correlates of certain basic perceptual phenomena may be found in D. N. Robinson: *J. exp. Psychol.*, 1966, *71*, 16–25. For EEG correlates of human learning, see especially W. G. Walter, R. Cooper, V. J. Aldridge, W. C. McCallum, and A. L. Winter: *Nature*, 1964, *203*, 380–384.

4. The most recent systematic review of evoked response correlates of psychological processes can be found in E. Donchin and D. B. Lindsley (Eds.), *Average Evoked Potentials*, (Washington, D.C.: N.A.S.A., 1969).

5. Note: The foveal arrangement is usually a cone-bipolar-ganglion ratio of 3:2:3.

6. I've offered data from visual sensory codes for illustrative purposes. Coding of an analogous nature is found in all sensory systems. For *taste*, consult Y. Zotterman, pp. 205–216, in: *Sensory Communication*, W. Rosenblith (ed.), M.I.T. Press,

Cambridge, 1961. For impulse-coding in *hearing,* see I. Tasaki: *J. Neurophysiol.,* 1954, *17,* 97–122. By far the best of the earlier papers on *auditory* coding is that of R. Galambos & H. Davis: *J. Neurophysiol.,* 1943, *6,* 39–58. More recently, Y. Katsuki, T. Watanabe, & N. Suga: *J. Neurophysiol.,* 1959, *22,* 603–623. On the neural coding of *position sense,* see V. Mountcastle, G. Poggio, & G. Werner: *J. Neurophysiol.,* 1963, *26,* 807–834.

7. An excellent brief discussion of this issue and an introduction to modern theories of signal detection can be found in W. P. Tanner & J. A. Swets: *Psychol. Rev.,* 1954, *61,* 401–409.

# 5
# Engrams, Molecules, and Other Demons

At each level of biological organization, from single cells to entire organisms, we find the capacity to respond. The pores of our skin open to release wastes. The unicellular amoeba surrounds particles of food. The capillaries of a plant stem draw water up to the leaves and flowers. It is in these myriad responses that we discover the manner in which adaptation occurs. Survival requires response capacities to match the demands of environmental realities. But it is one thing to say that a response serves some purpose and quite another to say that the response is *purposive*. The distinction is clear when we discuss capillary action in the stem of a plant. We don't say that the stem is attempting to feed its flowers, that the stem is purposely trying to pass nutrients higher and higher. Rather, we explain the event as the outcome of basic physical processes that have the effect of opposing gravity. We call the response "capillary action." Similarly, when we gently rest a pin in water, we don't describe its failure to sink in terms of "swimming" but as an example of surface tension. We reject out of hand the notion that the pin is trying to do anything. It is simply responding according to fixed physical laws. Consciousness is not necessary, nor is it invoked for explanatory purposes. With the amoeba, most of us feel every bit as comfortable in rejecting purposivity. A food particle partially dissolves in solution and changes the chemical environment surrounding the amoeba. On some macromolecular basis, the constituents of the amoeba attract and are attracted by the constituents of the medium. The response is analogous to the photochemical decomposition occurring within the retina in the presence of light. The rods and cones don't "see"; they respond. They don't *act;* they *react.* Any explanation of such behavior need not go beyond the principles of physics and chemistry.

Now let us examine a child approaching a radiator for the first time. He runs across the room to fetch a toy on the windowsill behind the radiator. As he reaches for it, his arm touches the radiator, he jumps back, lets out a cry, and is momentarily arrested by pain. Later, with the toy in the same place, the child walks toward it gingerly. He lifts his arm well above the radiator, carefully extends his grasp, clutches the toy, slowly withdraws his arm, and finally moves quickly beyond the range of the heat. At a "common-sense" level, we say that the child has *learned* not to touch a hot radiator. What does this mean? How does *action* differ from *reaction?* At what point in the series of events are physical laws no longer sufficient? Which of the steps requires consciousness? What has the child done that is different from the amoeba?

## LEARNING

Contrary to expectation, it is not at all easy to specify how the behavior of the child differs from that of the amoeba. We can ask the child why he is acting the way he is and receive the answer "I hurt myself on that." But the fact that the child can offer an account while the amoeba cannot doesn't really address itself to the question of fundamental differences in function. A deaf mute, for example, cannot tell us why he is reacting the way he does. Are we to conclude that learning only occurs when the organism tells us it does? Clearly not. It makes just as little scientific sense to suggest that learning occurs when an organism "knows" it has learned; for then we have the problem of defining "to know."

The progress of science is marked by our ability to create simplicity out of chaos, order out of diversity. No two events in nature are exactly alike. And yet, despite the apparent differences, we can include large numbers of diverse events under a small collection of laws. The planets in no way resemble grasshoppers. But the laws of gravity are indifferent to the differences and, at a certain level, actually eliminate them. Can we treat *learning* the same way? That is, can we agree on a definition of learning that is largely insensitive to the staggering diversity of forms it may take? Let us try.

First of all, let us stipulate that learning involves or at least allows *new* behavior, behavior that is different from that which occurred before conditions allowing learning were created. The difference may be in the *frequency* with which behavior occurs, its *strength,* the sequence or order of responses, its duration—in short, any *measurable* aspect of behavior. But difference is not enough. For example, a man who loses a leg will walk less frequently, for shorter periods of time, with less even strides, etc. We do not want to call these differences *learning.* First of all, they are essentially not modifiable, whereas we know intuitively that learned behavior can be changed. That is, the differences resulting from learning can also become different or changed. To embrace this intuition, we must add the criterion of *reversibility.* Thus, we begin our definition by describing learning as a reversible alteration of behavior. Can we get the child to walk more quickly toward the radiator after he has been burned? Can we get him to behave with greater confidence; that is, with greater speed, accuracy, frequency? If so, we can say that learning initially involves greater caution but that, with training (further learning), the cautious behavior can be modified. Now let us ask the same question of the amoeba. Can we get it to move *away* from food? Can we get it to envelop a chemically "neutral" substance? As it happens, we can't. The amoeba's behavior is described as *tropistic.* Tropisms are total bodily orientations toward or away from a stimulus. The positive (toward) and negative (away) tropisms are not reversible. They occur with the very first presentation of the relevant stimulus. Within the physiological limitations of the organism, they are inexhaustible. Learning, on the other hand, is both reversible and gradual. It involves a *progressive* modification of behavior and does not appear with the first presentation of the stimulus or event to be learned. The flowers that bend toward the sun can not be trained to lean away from it. Nor do they require repeated exposures in order to bend correctly. They may, however, have to reach a certain degree of maturity before this phototropic response occurs.

Herein lies another necessary characteristic of learning: It must be distinguished from *maturation,* which also may lead to progressive changes in behavior and may even be reversible (for instance, in senility). Some highly adaptive behavior requires no training for its appearance. Robins build nests without practice. Salamanders swim as soon as the structures necessary for swimming have matured. These behaviors are innate in the sense that practice is not necessary. They are *triggered* rather than *nurtured* by the environment. *Reflexes* are illustrative. The child *learned* to approach the radiator slowly, but he did not "learn" to withdraw his arm when it was burned. That event occurred as soon as the stimulus was applied, in the absence of any practice; it would, in fact, have occurred if the spinal nerves alone were involved. Reflexes are to parts of the body what tropisms are to the entire body. As changes in behavior, they are neither progressive nor reversible.

From what has been said, we may accept as a tentative (and arbitrary) definition of learning the following: "Learning is a progressive and reversible change in behavior—a change that is not attributable to maturation alone." If we wish to make the foregoing even more rigorous and perhaps more revealing, we might also distinguish learning from instinctive behavior: "Learning is a nonheritable, progressive, and reversible change in behavior—a change that is not attributable to maturation alone."

## THE CONDITIONED REFLEX

Since Aristotle, scholars have speculated on the role of repetition in learning, on the formation of "associative bonds" between events presented together frequently. It was Ivan Pavlov (1849–1936), however, who first attempted to build a scientific psychology on the foundation of philosophical associationism. Pavlov never had much patience with psychology, which in his day was far more mentalistic

**FIGURE 5-1**
Ivan Pavlov (1849–1936). (The Bettmann Archive.)

and far less experimental than it is now. He argued strongly for a biopsychology, a biology that would include the problems of psychology in its subject matter; and he rejected the possibility that, when all physiological processes are understood, unexplained psychological characteristics will still remain. His research on the conditioned reflex, in his view, furnished empirical support for this essentially philosophical position.

Everyone knows of Pavlov's dogs, trapped in a harness, with powdered food placed in their mouths each time a tone was sounded. After a few presentations, the tone was sufficient to elicit a salivary reflex. Pavlov called salivation occurring in the presence of food an *unconditioned reflex,* or an unconditioned response (UCR), because it is not conditional upon training of any kind. The food, because it is unconditionally capable of producing salivation, is an *unconditioned stimulus* (UCS). The tone, on the other hand, is a *conditioned stimulus* (CS), because its ability to produce salivation is conditional upon its being paired with the appropriate UCS. Salivation to the tone, then, is a *conditioned response* (CR), which occurs only after frequent pairings of UCS and CS. Somehow, after frequent enough pairings, the CS (tone) comes to function as if it were the UCS (food). This effect, according to Pavlov, is the result of *stimulus substitution;* that is, the CS now serves as a substitute for the UCS. The sequence of events in a Pavlovian conditioning study is shown in Figure 5-2. He in-

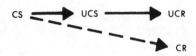

*FIGURE 5-2*
Sequence of events in Pavlovian conditioning.

ferred from the facts of reflex conditioning that all so-called psychological functions are but physiological events. In this sense, the experimental animal—the dog secured to the Pavlov frame—was but a biological system whose response properties were determined by the physical effects of stimulation. The CS comes to control reflexive behavior by *substitution;* i.e., it comes to be treated *as if* it were the UCS because it has been presented often in conjunction with the UCS.

## Explanatory Limitations of Conditioned Reflex Concept

Now, by what means is Pavlov's *stimulus substitution* achieved? That is, what kind of a machine is required to treat the CS as if it were the UCS? Let us look at an example of Pavlovian conditioning with a human subject. Each time the word "tree" is announced, the subject is given a mild shock to his right palm. The sequence "tree" → shock is repeated, say, fifty times. Following the administrations of shock, the subject's heart rate increases. On the fifty-first trial, however, only the word "tree" is announced, and no shock is delivered. Yet, even in the absence of shock, the subject's heart rate increases. In Pavlovian terms, his heart rate has been conditioned to the CS ("tree"), which now serves as a substitute for the UCS (shock). On the fifty-second trial, the experimenter announces the word "bush." Sure enough, the "conditioned" increase in heart rate occurs. On the fifty-third trial, the test stimulus is the word "moon"; no CR is observed. On the fifty-fourth trial, the cue is "oak"; again, the CR occurs. What is demonstrated by all this is that the effective stimulus can be specified only in terms of *meaning*. That is, there is no *physical* continuum along which the values of the CS can be arranged. Indeed, there is no continuum at all. The stimulus substitutions are semantic substitutions, and this type of substitution requires the very kind of psychological organism that Pavlov was out to dismiss. Even the dog, who comes to substitute the sound of a bell for the presence of food in the mouth, is actively (perceptually) selecting certain elements from the entire stimulus domain and rejecting and ignoring others.

With semantic factors, the case against Pavlov's model is far more cogent, but even the bell-food substitution appears to require what, for want of a neutral word, must be called *mental* operations. For example, Pavlov observed that, during the conditioning procedure, the dog would adopt certain stereotyped behaviors prior to the presentation of the UCS. With the onset of the tone (or just before it), the dog's ears would prick, his posture would straighten, he would look in the direction of the food-delivering apparatus and otherwise engage in an ensemble of behaviors which Pavlov dubbed (in order to replace the mentalistic concept of attention) *the orienting reflex.* However, he did not explain why certain stimuli and not others became the focus of such responses. To answer by asserting, "Since the bell was followed by food, the bell acquired the power of eliciting the orienting reflexes" is to beg the question, since the very acquisition of that power depends upon the prior "mental" act of substitution, discrimination, evaluation, etc. Nor is the complaint dispelled completely by recourse to "adaptation" or "habituation" effects. According to this line of explanation, the total environment, minus the bell, is present during food absence as well as food presence. The ceiling of the laboratory, for example, is paired with the UCS for only a brief period; the rest of the time, it is not. The bell, however, is *always* correlated with the UCS. Accordingly, most (theoretically, *all*) environmental features *except the bell* come to serve as *conditioned inhibitors;* that is, they are correlated with the absence of a UCS. But, if this were true, the removal of any one of the features of the experimental environment should enhance the conditioning process. It should, according to the theory, *disinhibit* the CR. Of course, such "irrelevant" alterations have no such effect. Indeed, if the "conditioned" animal is removed to an entirely different environment (one that is presumably devoid of "habituating" elements), he should begin to salivate all over the place, or at least the magnitude of the CR should be increased. It isn't. Certain features of the total experimental environment are known to be effective in these regards; others, irrelevant. Again, it is not clear how "efficacy" and "relevance" can be specified independently, with no reference to psychological (perceptual, cognitive) characteristics of the dog.

The foregoing does not sum to the declaration that Pavlovian conditioning does not occur. What does seem clear is that such conditioning is not responsible for the effects attributed to it in the entire range of settings in which such effects are producible. Logically, it is by no means certain that Pavlov's uncompromisingly mechanistic conditioning is even possible; i.e., that a bona fide CR can be produced in a system devoid of psychological attributes. Operationally, there is no question but that the frequent pairing of stimuli which initially lack relevance with those that initially are biologically relevant will enhance the ability of the former to elicit behavior previously called forth by the latter. But, stated in this form, the concept of conditioning no longer poses a threat to mentalism. Instead, it is but a restatement of traditional empirical associationism.

Setting aside these logical considerations, Pavlov's theories fell on empirical hard times as well. Illustrative of the difficulties were those resulting from his attempt to provide a neurophysiological account of stimulus generalization.

### Empirical Limitations of Conditioned Reflex Concept

Pavlov showed that stimuli different from the CS but lying along the same physical continuum are also effective in eliciting a CR. If, for example, the dog was initially conditioned to salivate to a tone of

1,000 cps, he would also salivate to tones of other frequencies. However, as Figure 5-3 shows, the CR (salivation to tones) diminishes in strength as the tones get further away in frequency from the initial CS (1,000 cps). Pavlov referred to this "spreading" effect as *stimulus generalization.*

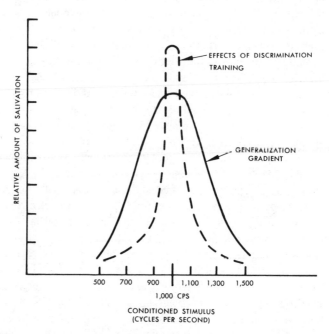

**FIGURE 5-3**
The conditioning of discrimination and generalization.

In an attempt to explain stimulus generalization, Pavlov proposed the mechanism of *cortical irradiation.* He assumed that each stimulus has a unique cortical location such that a 1,000-cps tone will excite one area while a 1,200-cps tone will excite an adjacent area. A given stimulus in Pavlov's view, will have its maximum effect in a specific region but will also influence immediately surrounding areas. Thus, a CS of 1,000 cps will also come to be represented, with diminishing strength, in cortical areas associated with tones similar in frequency. The proposed mechanism involved the spread of excitation with reduced strength at further and further distances from the cortical locus of the CS.

Pavlov accounted for the phenomenon of *discrimination* in similar fashion. Discrimination is the reverse of generalization. For example, if food is put in the dog's mouth after presentation of a 1,000-cps tone but not after a 1,050-cps tone, the dog eventually will salivate to 1,000 cps but not to 1,050 cps. A *conditioned discrimination* has been produced. According to the concept of cortical irradiation, the CS here is represented in cortical area *A*, the region excited by a tone of 1,000 cps. Area B, activated by the nonrewarding 1,050-cps tone, develops a *conditioned inhibition*, which is maximum at 1,050-cps and which spreads to neighboring cortical regions. Through the spread (irradiation) of excitatory and inhibitory currents, the data of generalization and discrimination are produced.

In his studies of conditioned discrimination, Pavlov observed that dogs required to make extremely fine discriminations often became hyperemotional. They would bark, bite, urinate, and otherwise behave in bizarre ways. He termed this behavior *experimental neurosis* and explained it in terms of irresolvable neurological conflicts; that is, the processes of excitation and inhibition are so thoroughly overlapping that adaptive behavior is impossible.

This first attempt to explain reflex learning (conditioning) in neurophysiological terms was brilliant but ultimately futile. In the first place, Pavlov's conditioned stimuli were limited mainly to two types only: (1) tones of different frequency, (2) tactile stimuli delivered to various parts of the body. For example, he would touch the foreleg of the dog and follow this with a shock in order to obtain conditioned flexion. Then, when this CR was firmly established, he would determine the effects of touching the shoulder, the back, the hind limbs, etc. True to the theory, the further removed the test stimuli were from the location of the original CS, the weaker or less frequent the CR. These effects were essentially the same as those obtained with tones. However, most stimuli do *not* arrange themselves in such orderly fashion along successive cortical areas. The body surface does reveal such *topographic organization;* a systematic shift in the region of cortical excitation for each systematic shift in the skin area stimulated; and, within broad limits, so does the auditory system. But other sensory dimensions (color, loudness, odor, pain) are not found to conform to such rigid geometric organizations. Yet, generalization and discrimination are every bit as much associated with these stimuli as they are with tones and touch. Quite simply, the functional anatomy required by the cortical irradiation hypothesis just does not exist.

An even more telling case against the theory is provided by the phenomenon of *transposition*. Someone who knows a melody well can easily recognize it no matter what key it is played in. Even though the actual sound frequencies change considerably from key to key, he is able to *transpose* these different keys and recognize the melody by the *relationship* among the notes. Animals perform analogous transpositions. If a monkey is rewarded each time he presses a key whose illumination level is, say, twenty units but is not rewarded when he presses one of ten units, he learns very quickly to respond to the twenty units. If he is then required to choose between a new illumination level of forty units and one of twenty units (the value at which all previous responses have been rewarded), he will respond to the forty-unit stimulus. That is, rather than learning the absolute (physical) value of the stimulus, the monkey has learned the relation *brighter than.* Any theory based upon the passive spread of excitatory currents will not be able to account for transposition, and Pavlov's certainly could not.

## STIMULUS-RESPONSE CONNECTIONISM

Pavlov's "reflex psychology" was the forerunner of American *behaviorism,* whose founder, John B. Watson (1878–1958), believed that all human behavior can be explained in terms of the accretion of conditioned reflexes. At the root of it, Watsonian behaviorism was little more than a modified neo-Cartesian materialism. Watson knew much more about nerves, reflexes, and physiology than did Descartes, but the general flavor of his theory was not very much different from what even the Ancients had recognized.

Modern behavioral psychology is far from what Watson promoted in 1912, but it does retain the notion that learning, in the final analysis, is a connection (if only in *time*) between some feature of the environment (stimulus) and some aspect of behavior (response). The simplest model designed to explain the process assumes that afferent signals become connected to appropriate efferent fibers such that, in the presence of a particular stimulus, a given (conditioned) response is initiated. It was Pavlov's hypothesis that the connections occur in the cerebral cortex, a proposition supported by the near impossibility of obtaining conditioned responses in decorticate animals.

In order to develop the connectionist line of reasoning, we should examine the general organization of the cerebral cortex, as shown in Figure 5-4. The major "lobes" are indicated. The *parietal cortex* receives impulses from the body surface as well as from sensory structures imbedded within the muscles; thus, it is "in" the parietal cortex that we would expect to find the representation of touch, hot and cold, limb position. The auditory pathways project finally to the *temporal* cortex; the visual, to the *occipital* cortex. On each side of the fissure of Rolando (the Rolandic "strip") are regions associated with sensory (post-Rolandic) and motor (pre-Rolandic) functions. The

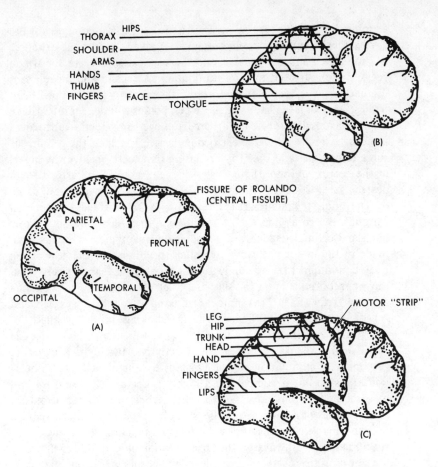

**FIGURE 5-4**
Gross cortical organization. (A) Major lobes of cortex. (B) Motor "strip" or "pre-Rolandic" cortex. (C) Sensory cortex (post-Rolandic). The amount of cortical area serving a particular part of the body does not depend upon the actual size of the body part. Rather, the greater the mobility (for motor cortex) or sensitivity (for sensory cortex) of the region, the greater is the cortical area devoted to it. For example, a good amount of motor cortex is devoted to the thumb and fingers, the lips and the tongue. Sensory cortex is disproportionately represented by lip and finger areas.

latter are controlled by the motor cortex, the area stimulated by Fritsch and Hitzig one hundred years ago. The sensory strip occurs at the anterior margin of the parietal lobe.

The various lobes and regions of the cortex receive fibers from numerous *subcortical* structures. There are two popular methods of determining which subcortical structure projects to which region of the cortex. The first is electrophysiological. A given subcortical structure is stimulated, and we hunt around the cortical surface to see which regions are activated by this stimulation. A second and more exact method involves *neural degeneration*. If we destroy a collection of cell bodies (nucleus), the axons of these cell bodies will degenerate. Since it is the axons that project to the cortex, we can select a subcortical structure, destroy it by electrocoagulation, sacrifice the animal at some later time, and then, by preparing thin sections, layer by layer, of the cortex, observe the course of degeneration. Similarly, we can destroy a portion of the cortical surface and, using the same degeneration technique, trace the *descending* cortical projections. Through the combined use of stimulation and recording on the one hand and cellular-degeneration studies on the other, a map has been made of the major pathways by which the brain and the rest of the body communicate. The connectionist theories of learning rely upon this neural organization for support. Such theories require (a) major sensory "trunk lines," (b) some interlinking or connecting device, and (c) major motor "trunklines." The interlinking device is called the *association cortex*. In primates especially, this association cortex is surprisingly silent during normal activity, although nonspecific responses to stimulation can be elicited. Presumably, these association areas do not participate in a highly specific way in sensory and motor functions but do serve to tie together the input and output signals. Learning theories of the stimulus-response variety require that specific sensory messages can become functionally connected to specific motor pathways, so that presentation of a stimulus will excite the appropriate response. Learning, in this scheme, is but the accumulation of *S-R* connections.

## THE SHATTERING OF S-R CONNECTIONISM: CONTRIBUTION OF LASHLEY

One of the most inventive minds in neuropsychology was possessed by Karl Lashley, (Figure 5-5) who, from 1917 until his death in 1958, published more seminal ideas and valuable data than any figure since Pavlov. We will confront his genius again later. Here, we will examine only his treatment of the "connections."

Lashley called attention to "the problem of serial order" in neuropsychological theories of behavior. Consider, for example, the concert pianist. Orthodox connectionism offers this model to account for his virtuosity: He strikes key 1; as a result, sensory impulses from

**FIGURE 5-5**
Karl Lashley

his fingertip, from the muscles of his hand and arm, and from his ear all converge on appropriate cortical centers. This information is somehow integrated, and the product of this integration is delivered to the motor cortex; here, the proper signals are initiated which lead to the striking of key 2. In other words, each response creates sensory cues which come to determine the subsequent motor outflow.

The trouble with this model is that it cannot be applied to sequences of behavior that unfold with the rapidity witnessed in piano playing, speech, and numerous other performances. Assuming highspeed conduction (100 meters/sec), events at the fingertips would take about 10 msec to arrive at the cortex if only one synapse were involved. Since the pathways are *polysynaptic,* this act takes about 20–30 msec. Assuming that only negligible time is involved in decoding and in transferring the decoded information to the motor cortex, another 20–30 msec are required to transmit information from the motor cortex back to the fingers. Some 40–60 msec have now elapsed, and this is an *extremely* conservative estimate. But granting even this brevity, we still find that a professional pianist can play errorlessly compositions involving sequences of notes separated by less than 40–60 msec. Quite obviously, note 2 is struck *before* the sensory consequences of striking note 1 can affect the outcome.

Lashley then sought to determine whether specific afferent-efferent links are necessary for learning. In this connection, he noted that the motor cortex can be ablated, thus paralyzing the limbs on the opposite side, but that function will be restored postoperatively after a sufficient recovery period (usually, a matter of weeks). In one of his studies, he ablated the left motor cortex of a monkey. As a result, the monkey was incapable of moving his right arm; in fact, no impulses from cortex to spinal efferents could occur. The animal was then trained to withdraw his left arm to avoid a shock or, in another experiment, to reach for the correct of two stimuli in order to obtain food. Lashley then ablated the right motor cortex. As a result, the animal could no longer use the "trained" (left) limb. Soon, however, function returned to the right arm. Lashley then tested to see whether this limb could perform the tasks that had been learned by the other. Sure enough, the monkey was able to use his once-paralyzed limb to avoid shock or to obtain food—even though, during initial training, the paralyzed limb had shared none of the efferent commands involved in activity by the limb on the other side. Thus, the learning of an association does not require a *specific R* in the *S-R* sense.

Next, Lashley attacked the *S*. He trained animals to discriminate between two different visual stimuli; during training, however, the animals had one eye blindfolded. In other words, only one optic nerve was participating in the learning. Once the task had been learned to criterion, Lashley uncovered the blindfolded eye and blindfolded the "educated" eye. The animal had no difficulty whatever in executing the appropriate discriminative response. Thus, the *S* involved in the original learning (activity in the left optic nerve) was entirely absent in the nerve tested after learning had occurred. Clearly, learning does not require specific sensory-motor connections. Something more general and more *central* (i.e., the brain) is involved.

## CORTICAL CONNECTIONISM

In a now famous article, *In Search of the Engram*,[1] Lashley whimsically described his decades of searching for the *engram;* that is, the biological code, the neural or biochemical representation of whatever it is the animal has learned. If we agree that an organism has learned something and that the brain is essential to this process, then the learned information (the engram) must be somewhere in the brain and therefore should be surgically removable. The experimental steps that follow from such a view are these: (a) Train the animal to perform behavior $X$ (e.g., choosing squares rather than triangles in a discrimination task). (2) Perform a series of ablations, allowing the animal to recover from each before performing the next; after each operation, test the animal's retention. If failure ensues, test to see whether the animal can be retrained.

There are numerous variations on this theme. Usually, many animals are used, with a different region of the brain removed in different groups of them. Since the search is for the engram, the experimenter must make sure that the deficits he obtains are the result of a failure to learn or remember rather than the outcome of sensory and/or motor incapacities. For example, in the form-discrimination task, the animal will surely fail to perform correctly after his visual cortex is removed, since he is now *blind*. Instead of removing what has been learned, the surgeon has merely destroyed one structure necessary for the animal to sense the stimuli. Thus, a number of control operations become essential. If, for example, an investigator wants to be sure that the occipital cortex, while absolutely necessary for visual functions, is not involved in learning, he must select a learning task that does not require vision. The animal may be required to turn left when a high tone is presented and right when a low one is presented, in order to avoid shock. Once the animal has learned these responses, both sides of his occipital cortex are removed. Then, after an appropriate convalescent period, the animal is retested on the task and performs as well as before the ablation. Conclusion: The occipital cortex is not involved in the learning of pitch discriminations.

Lashley performed many studies of the type just described, using various learning and memory tasks and performing an assortment of ablations. From these tireless efforts, he could offer only the following general conclusions: (1) Learning is not represented in any specific and circumscribed region of the cerebral cortex. (2) Deficits following the surgical removal of cortical tissue depend far more on the *amount* removed than upon the particular locus. (3) Even when postoperative deficits ensue, they can usually be liquidated by retraining. His first conclusion made untenable any strict *localization* hypothesis in accounting for the neural basis of learning and memory. His second conclusion supported his concept of *mass action,* the notion that the brain *as a whole* participates in functions as complex as learning and memory. His third conclusion lent some credence to his theory of *equipotentiality;* that is, certain specific structures may serve specific cognitive functions, but other structures can come to serve the same functions when the primary areas have been destroyed or removed.

## The Engram and Delayed-Response Tasks

More recent studies suggest that Lashley's conclusions, although in the right direction, were somewhat overstated. In the first place, he conducted experiments of a certain type and not others. After all, any selection of learning tasks is bound to be arbitrary, and no man—not even Lashley—could hope, in one lifetime, to investigate every conceivable variety of learning and perform every possible surgical procedure. Moreover, Lashley spent nearly all his time in the cerebral cortex and thereby left the rest of the brain to neuropsychological posterity. As we shall see, the parts he left are in many respects more interesting than the ones he removed. Even within the cortex, his choice of learning tasks prevented him from discovering the importance of the prefrontal cortex. If it is destroyed, the animal is unable to learn a *delayed-response task.* In one such experiment, a monkey is shown a bit of food and then observes the food being placed under one of two or more boxes. After a delay of a number of seconds, the animal is released to approach the boxes. With lesions in anterior frontal cortex, the monkey cannot select the appropriate box; in the absence of a delay, however, he has no difficulty whatever.[2]

Initially, this finding was used to support the contention that the anterior frontal cortex is responsible for short-term memory. Subsequent studies suggest more complex relations. If, for example, the delay elapses with the animal in darkness, performance is significantly enhanced, suggesting that *attention* may be the process degraded by the operation.[3] Severe starvation also leads to improved performance, indicating the role of *motivational* variables. Thus, the anterior frontal cortex has a unique function in the delayed-response problem, although the exact nature of this function (learning, memory, motivation, attention?) is not clear. This example of the anterior frontal cortex underscores two important points: (1) Whether or not a specific function is achieved through the operations of a particular structure depends upon how that function is defined and the tests employed to measure it. (2) There is little reason to conclude in advance that a given structure serves one and only one function. In research of this kind, no matter how keen and careful the investigator may be, arbitrariness abounds. There is first arbitrariness of *task* variables. Why should delayed-response tasks be measures of memory? Perhaps, during the delay, the animal is distracted by other cues. Then there is the arbitrariness of *treatment* variables. Why ablate the anterior frontal cortex? Why not the parietal lobes too? Why not section the ventral roots of the cord? The answer to the latter question is "Without the ventral roots intact, the animal will not be able to move; therefore, even if he can *learn*, we will never see the results of this learning." But how can we be sure that the failure of the frontally ablated animal to perform the delayed-response task is also not the result of motor rather than cognitive deficits?

At some point, the investigator must accept the inevitability of arbitrariness in all research, make a good guess, and proceed. When he has finished, he looks at the results and decides whether to go further or to abandon the project. This decision, too, is an arbitrary one.

### Distribution of the Engram

The failure of specific ablations to remove specific learned habits led to the conclusion that the engram of any *S-R* association is probably distributed widely throughout the cortex. Of the many experiments forcing such a view, one is worthy of special attention.[4] In this experiment, monkeys were trained to make four separate discriminations: to select the brighter of two lights, the heavier of two weights, the higher of two tones, and one visual pattern rather than another. Each of these discriminations is mediated by defined regions of the cerebral cortex. After the animals had learned all four discriminations, the association cortex surrounding the four primary cortical areas involved in these four sensory abilities was ablated. Tests conducted after surgery indicated that all four discriminations had been lost. An extensive retraining program was then initiated to get the monkeys once again to discriminate the heavier of two weights. No other training was administered. However, once the monkeys had relearned the weight problem, they were tested on the other three discriminations. Oddly, the monkeys now were able to perform the other three discrimination tasks as well. Somehow, the relearning of one of the tasks equipped the brain *as a whole* to participate in problem solving that involved abilities not directly improved by training.

Once we accept the notion that the engram enjoys diffuse representation, we begin to look not for the location of what has been learned and remembered but for *processes* that might serve as the "code" for the experience. Given the known physiology of the brain, two possibilities come to mind immediately: *electrical* codes and *chemical* codes.

### The Engram as a "Circuit"

In the 1940s, the proposal was offered that learning involves the establishment of reverberating electrical circuits. Presumably, sensory impulses trigger a number of responses, and some of these responses lead to satisfying circumstances. For example, of the many responses a dog makes to a stimulus such as a food dish (salivation, rapid breathing, vocalization, tail wagging, sniffing, approach behavior, etc.), only some bring him directly into contact with the food. The neural representation of this $S-R$ connection takes the form of a circuit—something like an afferent-efferent link—that persists electrically. Initially (before conditioning), connections are loosely formed; and, since some of these connections are genetically laid down, unconditioned reflexes as well as certain instinctual behaviors exist. According to this theory, however, new connections, new cell assemblages, must be pieced together if learning is to occur. The assemblage need not be a structural connection, since there is virtually no new growth of neural tissue after birth or early infancy. Rather, the assemblage is a *functional* connection in that neighboring units that once had little or no dependence upon each other now participate communally in providing a response to stimulation. The proponents of this theory could not specify the precise mechanisms involved in this functional assembly; they simply inferred or hypothesized that learning involves the establishment of interneural dependencies and that, once established, these functional connections persist in the form of a recurring or reverberating circuit of electrical activity.

The last word is not in on these reverberating circuits. Some data have been offered to refute their existence. It is possible, for example, to reduce the body temperature of an organism to the point at which all electrical activity in the nervous system is terminated. The animal can be revived after this and, it is averred, restored to normal health. Rats have been conditioned, frozen, thawed, and retested. The principal finding is that learned behavior persists even after a period of prolonged freezing, during which no electrical activity in the CNS is possible.[5] One interpretation of this finding is that, since all electrical activity has been terminated, any existing "reverberatory circuit" has also been eliminated; therefore, according to the theory, learning should have been irretrievably lost. This, however, is not the only interpretation. We could just as well contend that, once formed, the circuit will return with all of the other electrical activity when normal conditions are reestablished. The fact that the animal can be restored to normal functioning after freezing indicates that whatever was going on before the freezing has somehow returned after the thaw.

A more direct test of the circuit hypothesis involves the active dissolution of ongoing electrical activity in the brain. This can be achieved by the administration of *electroconvulsive shock* (ECS). If a high-voltage source is connected to the two ears of an experimental animal and a strong shock is administered, the ongoing EEG is thrown into chaotic disruption. The animal loses "consciousness," the brain struggles through an episode of stormy seizure, and exhaustion follows. From the records of brain activity, it would appear that no "circuit" could withstand the crisis. Depending upon the intensity and duration of the ECS, the animal can be incapacitated anywhere from minutes to hours. Studies involving ECS take many forms,[6] but most of them reduce to a similar paradigm. The animal is given one or a several training trials until he has satisfied a learning criterion (for instance, jumping over a barrier when a tone is presented in order to avoid a shock that reliably follows the tone by two seconds). Once this learning has taken place, the animal is given an ECS. It may be presented immediately or at intervals of variable duration. Following ECS, the animal is allowed to recover and is then retested.

ECS research has produced widely varying results. The reported intervals over which ECS impairs previous learning have ranged from 10 seconds to more than 24 hours. Thus, the hypothesis that ECS, by disrupting neuroelectric circuits, produces a retrograde amnesia (failure to recall events just preceding the trauma) must be questioned on the basis of the variability of the findings. The ECS itself has aversive properties, and these alone may reduce the likelihood of the behavior that precedes ECS administration. Some studies purport to separate the aversive effects of ECS from the "amnesia" effects, but these are not convincing. Furthermore, most of the ECS studies have employed such simple learning tasks (stepping off a platform, jumping over a barrier, pressing a bar) that it has been difficult to determine whether the deficits following ECS are of a mnemonic nature or involve such faculties as perception, motivation, and attention. Suppose, for example, we place a rat on a pedestal in the center of a cage. In such situations, the rat usually hops off and begins to explore the surroundings. As he does, we administer a shock to the paws. To escape the shock, the rat must jump back on the pedestal. Moreover, after he has been shocked a few times, there is a marked tendency to remain on the pedestal. If, however, following the shock, the animal receives ECS, this tendency to remain on the pedestal dissipates, and the animal once again hops off and explores the terrain. If the interval between the shock and ECS is varied from 0.5 seconds to 30 seconds, we find that the tendency to avoid the floor is least at the shortest intervals. Beyond 10 seconds, ECS seems to have little effect on the aversive consequences of foot shock. These results have been interpreted to mean that, up to 10 seconds, ECS produces an "amnesia" for the foot shock; the rat "forgets" that shock is delivered when he hops off the pedestal. But could we not also argue that ECS diminishes the animal's sensitivity to pain, so that there is not as great an aversion to the shock as there had been? Could it be that, at short intervals, the ECS serves to make the rat hyperexcitable, so that, once placed on the pedestal, he tends to jump off quickly? Perhaps at the shortest intervals the ECS reduces the brain's response to punishment and, paradoxically, converts the foot shock into a "pleasurable" event.

Some of these alternatives are offered only half seriously, but they do underscore the challenge confronting one who wishes to make sense of studies of this kind. Is jumping off a stand even an example of "learning"? What we need, of course, is a task involving many separate steps during which ECS may be introduced in an attempt to cut the "link" at different points along the chain. We would want a task that cannot be learned unless steps 1,2,3,4 . . . n have been completed and, especially, a task in which the animal cannot begin at 2 or 5 or proceed from *n* to 1. Thus, if an animal—no matter how well he has learned the chain—receives ECS after step 3, on recovery he should not be able to begin at step 4. Step 3 could involve, for example, a light: if *blue,* turn left; if *green,* turn right. A blue light is presented; the animal turns left and proceeds down a long runway. Five, ten, or *n* seconds down the runway, ECS is delivered. After recovery, the animal is placed again at step 3, but the signal is not presented; that is, the animal must "remember" what color was used. The steps can be increased, compounded by additional cues, and demanding multiple responses. In such contexts, we may learn more about exactly what is happening to learned behavior when ECS is administered. For now, we can say only that when an animal is thrown into a state of convulsion, behavior is affected, and the behavior affected most seems to be that which was occurring just prior to the convulsion.

### The Engram and Long-Term Memory

Even if the confusion in the area of ECS research were dissolved and we had good reason to assume that the effects were indeed upon memory, we would still be left with the fact that ECS has no effect upon long-term memories. The rat who may have "forgotten" that his feet were just shocked when he jumped off the pedestal has no trouble finding his food cup or, for that matter, performing tasks he learned yesterday. Presumably, ECS can disrupt only recently formed circuits. Thus, the coding of recent information may be of a different nature than that involved for more distant events; that is, perhaps the short-term code is gradually transformed into a more durable engram. This, in fact, is the current thinking and, for several reasons, it seems that the long-term coding is of a *chemical* nature. First, the failure of ECS to disrupt information learned just minutes earlier suggests that this older information is not stored electrically. If it were, the convulsions should disturb the patterns and thus distort recall. Second, the history of ablative surgery, with few exceptions, indicates that specific memories do not reside within specific regions of the brain but, instead, are represented broadly. This fact alone would force our attention to the kind of mechanism that enjoys broad representation—a *chemical* one. Finally, the great successes in molecular biology with the DNA code for "genetic memory" have led many to conclude that a similar chemical code may exist for "experiential memory." This perspective soon gave rise to the question "What is the memory molecule?" The innocence of this question was quickly brought home as the data started coming in— particularly the data from studies involving RNA.

As molecules go, RNA (ribonucleic acid) is big and—unlike DNA, which is very stable—can be modified without much effort. Given the great structural stability of DNA, early workers tended to dismiss it as a "memory molecule," since the coding of life's experiences would require a chemical substance capable of taking on a number (a *large* number) of different configurations. DNA does have the capacity to take on an awesome number of different configurations. The specific configuration is set genetically and, once set, is apparently immutable. If the coded DNA in our cells changed as a result of our experiences, we would be able to pass our experiences on to subsequent generations genetically; that is, acquired characteristics would be heritable. For better or for worse, this does not happen. Barring mutations due, for example, to radiation, the genetic code (DNA) present at the time of the fertilization of the egg retains its specific nature throughout the lifetime of the organism. This very stability would prevent the DNA from serving as a flexible structure which, by adopting varied configurations, could code our experiences.

RNA is also a complex molecule, but it does not retain its chemical configuration as unfailingly as does DNA. Its chief responsibility is the manufacture of a variety of proteins—each different protein requiring a different RNA configuration. With RNA thus looking like a good bet, researchers began to measure RNA production in the brains of animals trained to perform different tasks. In one of the more frequently cited studies,[7] mice were required to balance themselves on a wire. (Is this *learning?*) After a period of exercise of this type, cells in the vestibular nucleus (Deiter's cells) were assayed for RNA concentration. Sure enough, the "balancing act" was followed by significant changes in the amount of RNA in these cells and in the supporting glial cells in the same area. Despite the fulfillment of the prophesy, however, only one conclusion here makes any sense; namely, that activity in a brain region increases the need for nutrients in that region and that protein, as the major nutrient, demands increased RNA for its production. The same investigators monitored the vestibular nucleus at the same time and found the presence of higher oxidation rates as well. Might we then conclude that $O_2$ is the memory molecule?

In other studies, involving the prevention of RNA synthesis during or just after training, chemicals that preclude the formation of RNA have proved to be correlated with learning and memory deficits. However, animals so treated may come to perform normally if extensive time elapses between training and tests of retention; that is, retention may suffer shortly after the introduction of an RNA inhibitor, but these "lost" memories "return" several weeks after the last administration of the inhibitor. We might conclude, then, that the effects are not on memory at all but on what may be called *retrieval;* that is, access to and utilization of stored information. It is a finding that reminds one of the "reminiscence" effect in Pavlovian conditioning. If, after conditioned responses have been established, the animal is exposed to trials on which the US never follows the response, extinction ensues; the CS is no longer successful in eliciting the CR. However, 24 hours after the first extinction session, there is a substantial increase in the frequency and magnitude of conditioned responses. During the "rest" interval following early extinction, there has occurred a restoration of conditioned behavior. Such "reminiscence" is usually treated as the weakening of an inhibitory process, and it may well be that RNA is uniquely important to the mechanisms responsible for inhibition.[8]

An apparently more conclusive test of the molecular hypothesis of memory has caused recent excitement.[9] It is a common observation that rats, given their druthers, tend to remain in the dark. Their vision isn't especially good, their olfaction is superb, and in the dark they enjoy considerable advantages over both prey and predator. However, rats are adaptable and, if shocked each time they enter the darker of two compartments, will come to spend most of their time in the lighted alternative, an exemplary wisdom displayed by all surviving species. The conditioning procedure is correlated with the formation of an identifiable neurochemical substance not present to the same degree in "naive" rats. Indeed, the substance can be synthesized. The dramatic finding is that when this substance is injected into the brains of untrained rats, they quite unnaturally come to avoid the dark. The substance has been given the name *scotophobin* (Greek: *scotos* = dark; *phobia* = fear), although whether or not "fear" has anything to do with the behavioral consequences is a question for pure speculation. Nonetheless, what more could we ask for? A conditioning procedure results in the formation of a neurochemical substance, which, when given to unconditioned animals, results in the kind of behavior that initially required training. Conclusion: The acquired fear of darkness has been coded chemically, and this "memory molecule" is sufficient to pass on the learning to untrained animals. Well, not necessarily or, at least, not yet. To begin with, we haven't the merest notion of why the "conditioned" rats avoided the dark. I don't know what the rat "feels" any more than I know if a bulb "feels" warm when the light's turned on. All I know is that when I do *"X,"* the rat comes to do "Y." So much for the *phobin* in scotophobin. There is yet another scenario. Conditioned avoidance may lead to the buildup, say, of a toxic substance that excites the tissues of the eyes to produce painful stimulation in darkness. In other words, the conditioning does lead to chemical alterations, but these are of an aversive rather than of a mnemonic nature; once injected into a naive animal, they produce pain when that animal enters the dark. Let's think of yet another explanation. The scotophobin may be simply a tranquilizing agent that inhibits the emotional cues initially responsible for the animal's escape from light. The rat is now quite comfortable in the lighted area and, given its reinforcement history, has no excuse for remaining in the dark. We could go on, but the point has been made. Before we can call RNA, proteins, or any other substance a "memory molecule," several *minimum* criteria should be satisfied.

1. The chemical substances must undergo measurable changes in all instances in which learning has been observed to occur.

2. Elimination or neutralization of the substance prior to training should make learning impossible, since learning depends upon the storage of immediately preceding events.

3. Elimination or neutralization of the substance should lead to measurable impairments of memory and, when complete, to complete losses of memory.

4. Since recall is impaired by the acquisition of new information

that is similar to but different from what has been learned, the chemistry purported to code memory must be similarly influenced.

5. The well-established phenomena of generalization and discrimination must be possible, given the chemical model that is proposed.

6. The chemical changes cited as codes of memory must be distinguishable from those resulting from mere exercise or changes in levels of activity.

7. The chemical changes cited as codes of memory must be distinguishable from those involved only in basic sensory or motor functions. For example, if we deny the animal access to oxygen, learning and memory are impaired—at least in part because the animal is dying, and death impairs, among other functions, learning and memory. Similarly, if the animal is taught a brightness discrimination and then the optic nerves are severed, "retention" is eliminated. Presumably, this is not because the animal has forgotten which stimulus is brighter but because he cannot see either of them.

Research on the chemistry of learning and memory has not yet been able to satisfy these criteria. As of now, we know that certain neurochemical substances are essential to learning and memory. This fact, however, in no way suggests that these substances *are* learning and memory.

Even if we accept the proposition that learned behaviors *must* be coded and stored chemically, only a small part of the problem of explaining learning and memory has been settled. Behavior requires, among other things, the initiation of movements. Impulses to the relevant muscles must be carried by the efferent fibers if contractions are to occur. Any chemical model of learning and memory must, therefore, indicate the manner in which (a) neuroelectric activity establishes the chemical code and (b) the chemical code leads to the initiation of those neuroelectric events necessary for behavior to occur. We need, in other words, both an electrochemical transducer stage and then a chemoelectric transducer stage. Moreover, these mechanisms are probably different from and much more complex than those involved in sensory transduction. The photopigments in rods and cones give rise to electrical events determined by physical properties of the light stimulus. Any appropriate photographic emulsion can do this, and we can even make photocells that simulate this kind of reaction. But with memory, the task is incredibly more demanding in that some *new* chemical or state is necessary for each nuance of our experience. And this new chemical must be able to lead to the appropriate pattern of impulses on the response side of the organism. Given the magnitude of the problem, excitement over the likes of scotophobin may be somewhat premature.

When we enter the laboratory, we are forced to leave outside most dimensions of the phenomenon we are trying to understand. We wish to learn the most basic processes involved, those that participate in *all* manifestations of the phenomenon, no matter how diverse they may be. At the beginning of this chapter, we constructed a definition of learning that was intended to include all events in which we believe learning occurs and to exclude all behaviors that we consider to be unlearned. We did not, however, specify the conditions necessary for learning to occur. Thus, while we agreed to what learning is, we omitted statements describing how it comes to pass. To fill in this gap, it may be instructive to imagine ourselves as hungry rats, dropped into a small box. There doesn't seem to be any food around; we sniff along the ceiling and in the corners—still no food. Wait! What's that thing sticking out of the wall? We almost tripped over it. Maybe if we stand on it we'll be able to look into one of the high corners. We step onto the bar, and a "click" occurs. Startled, we jump off, another "click" is heard, and a pellet of food drops into the small well under the bar. Clearly, the "action" is at this end of the cage. Now we feel the bar gently, then a little more forcefully, and—"click"—"click" and another pellet. Good. Let's press the bar. "Click"—"click"; one more pellet. Now we know. When the bar is pressed, food is delivered to the foodwell.

What actually is going on in the "mind" of the rodent is, of course, a mystery. But we know that when food has been withheld for a day or two, the rat does explore the cage, sniffs about, and sooner or later (even accidentally) presses the lever down. After the first pellet of food, the rat stays near the bar. After the second or third, he begins to press the bar regularly. Our definition of learning has been satisfied, and we also can say something about the conditions that abetted this performance. The fully sated rat also may press the bar, but the delivery of a pellet of food has a greatly reduced effect upon his subsequent behavior. He presses no more and no less whether food results or not. The bar-pressing behavior, to become reliable, must be followed by certain events. Psychologists refer to those events that increase the probability of the behavior preceding them as *reinforcers*. The term is intended to be neutral. The events are "reinforcers" not in the sense that "pleasure" or "pain" is produced but in the sense that they strengthen (make more frequent) a particular kind of behavior, the kind that leads to these events. We may hypothesize that a stimulus reinforces behavior because it leads to some condition that favors survival. But we have little trouble getting animals and some men to perform in ways that *threaten* survival. So, at best, the "survivalistic" explanation is limited. All we can say is that, usually, stimuli that remove conditions of biological "need" come to control behavior. The correct response is said to be *drive-reducing,* where, in our illustration, the "drive" is hunger. In most situations involving animal behavior, learning occurs most efficiently when basic biological drives (hunger, thirst, pain) have been established and when only the learned behavior will be successful in reducing them. If we add a requirement such as responding only in the presence of a blue light, the animal will "learn" to respond when blue is present and not when it is absent. That is, the animal will utilize those cues that signal the availability of reinforcing stimuli. The animal must learn which are the relevant ones. In order for him to do this, responses to irrelevant cues must be nonreinforced *(extinguished).*

If we are to understand learning and memory in neural terms, we must know something about these conditions of *drive* and *cue.* In different terms, we must know something about *motivation* and *attention.* What mechanisms are operative in the nervous system when drives have been established? How does the system come to treat relevant and irrelevant cues in a discriminative way? These are the topics of the next chapter.

## NOTES AND REFERENCES

1. K. S. Lashley, *In Search of the Engram,* pp. 454–482, in *Symp. Soc. exp. Biol.,* No. 4., (New York: Cambridge Univ. Press, 1950).

2. See, especially, M. Mishkin & L. Weiskrantz: *J. comp. physiol. Psychol.,* 1958, *51,* 276–281; K. H. Pribram, M. Mishkin, H. E. Rosvold, & S. J. Kaplan: *J. comp. physiol. Psychol.,* 1952, *45,* 567–575.

3. R. Malmo: *J. Neurophysiol.,* 1942, *5,* 295–308.

4. H. Kluver: *Biol. Symp.,* 1942, *7,* 263–264.

5. R. W. Gerard: *J. verb. Learn. & verb. Behav.,* 1963, *2,* 22–33.

6. The pioneering study was done by C. P. Duncan: *J. comp. physiol. Psychol.,* 1949, *42,* 32–44. See also S. L. Chorover & P. Schiller: *J. comp. physiol. Psychol.,* 1965, *59,* 73–78.

7. H. Hyden & E. Egyhazi: *Proc. Nat. Acad. Sci., U.S.,* 1962, *48,* 1366–1373.

8. A brief and simple review of this literature has been provided by E. M. Gurowitz in *The Molecular Basis of Memory* (Englewood Cliffs, N.J.: Prentice-Hall, 1969).

9. G. Ungar & L. N. Irwin: *Nature,* 1967, *214,* 453–455. An excellent critique of this entire area is given in chapter 9 of *The Biochemical Basis of Neuropharmacology* by J. R. Cooper, F. E. Bloom, and R. H. Roth (Oxford, 1970).

# 6
## Arousal, Attention, Appetites

Until the present century, views of the nervous system were highly linear and tended to follow the geometric lines first developed by Descartes. According to these early views, basic reflexes are controlled at the level of the spinal cord; and such "spinal behavior" was regarded as involuntary, fixed, largely all-or-nothing. At the next level, the *medulla oblongata* was held responsible for the reflexive behavior of specialized muscles—the diaphragm (breathing), cardiac muscle (heart rate), etc. Enveloping the medulla, the large lobes of the *cerebellum* participate in the regulation of movements. At still another level, the *midbrain* allegedly houses those structures that mediate certain sensory and motor activities. Then, finally, covering all of these structures, sitting atop as a great regulatory cloud, the cerebral hemispheres prevail. With higher and higher species, more and more elaboration of the cerebral cortex occurs—until, with man, the cortex comes to dominate the cranial volume. What could be more natural than the assumption that here in the mammoth cerebral mantle reside the unique capacities of reason, thought, memory, and consciousness itself? In man, the descending influences of the cerebrum control the "baser" "instincts." All "lower" functions are thus brought under the powers of cortical action.

This older view—which, as we shall see, was simplistic—had a good deal to recommend it. The most cursory inspection of brain development phylogenetically reveals a disproportionate expansion of the cortex at the expense of subcortical structures. In the frog, these subcortical structures (the "primitive brain") dominate; in higher and higher organisms, they shrink proportionately while the cortex thickens and spreads. Apparently, then, in the animal kingdom, the relative representation of the cerebral mass increases as the intellectual and rational faculties increase. Early clinical findings also seemed to support such a view. Injury to the cerebral mantle, these findings revealed, is inevitably accompanied by loss of those functions usually described as "higher": speech, memory, problem solving. Not only were subcortical structures unsuspected, but they were not easy to examine. Postmortem investigations were usually limited to the cortex; if something was found there, the autopsy was likely to end. Added to these considerations, research findings showed that in spinal animals (animals whose cords are transected so that communication between brain and body is impossible) only reflexes survive. And the *decerebrate* preparation (an animal whose cerebral connections to the remainder of the brain are severed by transection at the midbrain level) was reliably found to be rigid, unresponsive, and passive. Clearly, the data stood in support of the model: The mind resides in the cortex.

Gradually, however, discoveries mounted to challenge the concept of rigid levels of organization. Not only did clinicians begin to detect extremely complex consequences of subcortical disease, but electrical-stimulation studies demonstrated dramatically the extent to which the cortex is controlled by subcortical events. As Figure 6-1 shows, a diffuse band of interconnecting fibers ascends from the anterior lip of the medulla and proceeds forward to the "floor" of the

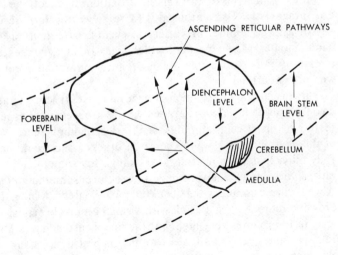

**FIGURE 6-1**
Reticular projection.

forebrain. In its passage, it sends fibers abundantly to regions of the *thalamus*. The thalamus, in turn, sends pathways up to the cortex. Some are distributed diffusely over large areas of cortex; others are focused on narrow regions of cortex. When the *reticular formation* is stimulated, its activity is reliably followed by activity of the cortex. That is, the electrical responses of cortical tissue are under the control of subcortical (reticular) events.[1] There is, then, a *reticulocortical projection system*. More specifically, when the reticular formation is stimulated, vast regions of the cerebral cortex undergo changes in their intrinsic rhythmic activity (EEG). High-amplitude rhythmic components give way to low-amplitude flurries of activity. This *desynchronization* of the EEG can be observed in animals and men under conditions of *arousal*. Should the sleeping cat receive stimulation to the reticular formation, he awakens immediately. Upon delivery of the stimulus, the slow, rhythmic "sleep" waves of the EEG disappear and are replaced by high-frequency discharges. Behaviorally, the animal is seen to crouch, prick his ears, widen his eyes, and otherwise engage in preparatory ("alert") responses. Because of these effects, scientists refer to these reticulo-cortical pathways as an *ascending reticular arousal system* (ARAS).[2]

## MECHANISMS OF AROUSAL AND ATTENTION

It is in the complex interplay of cerebral cortex, reticular formation, and sensory thalamic nuclei that the neural scientist hopes to find the mechanisms of arousal and attention. In effect, the two terms are antagonistic. To be aroused is to be *generally* alert, accessible to any of a large number or variety of events. Attention, on the other hand, implies a *specific* perceptual bias. In fact, concentrated attention often is responsible for our failure to miss an event to which we were not attending.

Any discussion of attention or arousal must, at some point, include a consideration of *memory*. When we are aroused by or especially attentive to a particular stimulus, we are responding to certain features of the environment at the expense of others. And we do not do this willy-nilly. Instead, our attention is caught by something in the stimulus, something we know or have seen before, something *meaningful*. A well-worn example is the "cocktail party" effect. A man stands in a crowded room, having a drink with a small group of friends. The noise level in the room is very high, but the man is attending to his friends' remarks and is essentially deaf to anything else in his surroundings. Suddenly someone in another group several feet away happens to mention his name; and, although he has heard nothing of their conversation up to this point, he hears his name mentioned, loud and clear. In other words, he has been able to filter out meaningless background activity, but with the introduction of something meaningful, his attention shifts immediately, and the distant message passes through his "filters" unimpeded.

Effects of this kind tell us two things about the mechanisms of attention. First, at any given time most of what is happening around us fails to enter our conscious awareness. Second, this filtering is not arbitrary; it is *selective*. To be selective, it must be influenced by memory.

If we examine Figure 6-2, we get some sense of the type of circuit that must be involved in attention (selective filtering). A stream of irrelevant stimuli impinges upon the sense organs. Much of this information is blocked by the passive filtering characteristics of the sense organs themselves. For example, ultraviolet radiation is not responded to by the retinal rods and cones. Sound frequencies above 20,000 cps are not responded to by the auditory apparatus. Those stimuli whose physical properties are compatible with the sensitivity of the sensory mechanisms are responded to, and these responses are

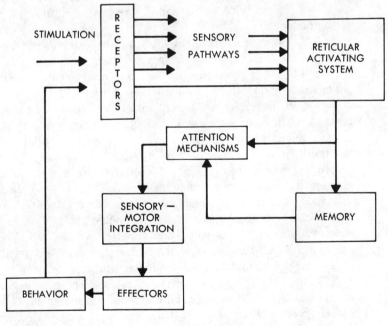

*FIGURE 6-2*
Boxes are not reality.

carried by the sensory nerves into the brain. At some early stage, the animal has to compare this information with past experiences. However, such comparisons cannot be made at the earliest stages, since survival requires the animal to respond to some kinds of stimulation before he has the time to determine what it is. For example, the child does not evaluate the temperature of a hot stove before removing his arm. Instead, he acts reflexively, and reflexes are indifferent to the memories of the organism.

There is provision for both arousal and attention in the projections from thalamus to cerebral cortex as well as in those from reticular formation to cortex. As indicated, certain thalamic nuclei project diffusely to extended regions of the cerebral cortex. Stimulation of these nuclei will have diffuse consequences analogous to those observed when an animal is aroused by external stimulation. Moreover, stimulation of ARAS also leads to EEG "arousal" patterns. Animals engaged in a visual-discrimination task perform more quickly and more accurately during electrical stimulation of ARAS. While direct evidence is not available, various studies suggest the following kind of arrangement:

1. External stimuli change in such a way as to activate ARAS.

2. Activity in ARAS "prepares" the cortex diffusely for subsequent inputs.

3. This preparation involves both motor and sensory functions (areas) of the cerebral cortex. In fact, sufficient stimulation of ARAS may lead to reflex responses (indiscriminate responses or responses not based upon qualitative features of the stimulus).

4. Signals in ARAS are shared with brain regions in which long-term memories are somehow coded. Pending this memory search, specific nuclei in the thalamus are activated by special reticulo-thalamic pathways. Perhaps, for example, as a result of memory search, the animal assigns greater "weight" to that aspect of the total stimulus flux that contains "blue light" (since "blue" has been paired with food so often that "blue" memories come to control further influences of ARAS on specific thalamic nuclei); in this instance, his generalized arousal gives way to specific attentiveness to the spectral properties of the stimulus. In such a circumstance, the animal may ignore changes in shape, distance, motion, brightness, etc.

5. If the animal is to correct unsuccessful responses, he must be able to shift attention to new or different stimulus elements. Thus, the consequences of his actions must become represented in memory in order for it to monitor in a flexible way the manner in which ARAS passes sensory signals on to thalamus and cortex.

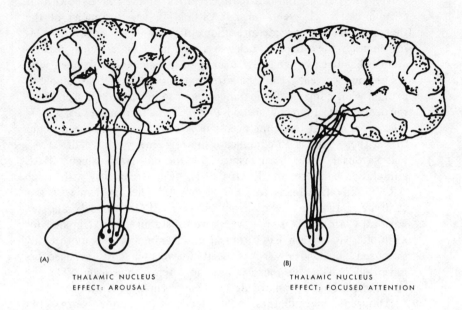

THALAMIC NUCLEUS
EFFECT: AROUSAL

THALAMIC NUCLEUS
EFFECT: FOCUSED ATTENTION

*FIGURE 6-3*
(A) Schematic illustration of diffuse thalamo-cortical projections. (B) Schematic illustration of specific thalamo-cortical projections.

Figure 6-3 illustrates these stages.

There is yet another function possible for the diffuse thalamo-cortical system. Repetitive low-frequency stimulation of those thalamic nuclei that project diffusely to cortex can induce sleep. In other words, this system can serve to *inhibit* the effects of both the reticular formation and the specific thalamo-cortical projections. We may infer that any system that can induce sleep—any system that can inhibit arousal—has satisfied one criterion for being considered part of an *attention* mechanism. In order for us to focus our attention, we must inhibit responses to all stimuli that are irrelevant to our purpose.

Given the anatomy of ARAS and both the specific and diffuse thalamic systems, we should be able to design an "attention" circuit. Once memory searches have singled out an appropriate stimulus and "weighted" it preferentially, the correct specific thalamic system is activated; at the same time, via the diffuse system, other areas of the cortex (or, perhaps, other specific thalamic nuclei) are silenced, at least relatively. Specifically what kinds of "loops" and circuits are involved when an animal is attentive? So far, studies have shown that certain electrical events in ARAS and in various nuclei of the thalamus reliably precede alterations of the animal's behavior.[3] Unfortunately, the range of behaviors examined under such circumstances has been very narrow, usually of the sleeping-waking variety. As of now, we really can't be sure that activity in ARAS is able to explain what happens, for instance, when someone is "aroused" by a musical composition, by an odd theory, by a loud noise, by a good idea. I doubt that the same events in ARAS can be used to account for all these states. To complicate matters, many studies of ARAS and "arousal" have been inspired by the ease with which ARAS stimulation can alter the EEG; that is, by the reliability with which ARAS activation leads to EEG "arousal." The problem with this strategy is that the relationship between EEG "arousal" and behavioral "arousal" is not very well established. Atropine, for example, will abolish EEG arousal in an animal who is quite easily "aroused" behaviorally.[4] And what do we mean by "aroused behaviorally"? That his muscles are more tense than usual? That he runs faster? That he is more alert to changes in his environment?

Different investigators have tended to define words like "alertness," "arousal," and "attention" in different ways. They have invaded different portions of ARAS. They have used different species or animals of different ages or animals with very different personal histories. They have employed broadly divergent tasks and peculiar stimulus configurations. It's little wonder that a "neuropsychology of attention" doesn't exist. What we do have is a catalog of several areas of the brain, which, when stimulated or removed or otherwise modified, reliably change what appears to be the alerting-attending behaviors of various animals. Indeed, with careful electrode placements, rats, cats, and monkeys can be awakened and put to sleep alternately, as if these two states were under the control of a valve. Removal of major portions of ARAS produces a somnolent animal, essentially unarousable. Chronic insomnia can be achieved by similar methods. But far more research is necessary, and much greater care in defining terms and procedures must be exercised if these phenomena are to become translated into a body of knowledge. Again, we must recognize the difference between a body of knowledge and a collection of facts.

## NEEDS, DRIVES, APPETITES

When we describe attention as the filtering of irrelevant stimuli and the enhancement of relevant stimuli, we must assume that "relevance" is either built into the system (e.g., the frog's "bug detector") or that it comes to be "built in" by experience. But *experience* is a broad term. We are literally bathed in stimulation, and we "experience" only a small fraction of the total. Those stimuli that are meaningful or relevant are said to enjoy this feature by virtue of their pleasurable or aversive consequences. We do not need modern behavioral psychology to tell us that most animals will attempt to secure food when hungry, or will labor to avoid shock, or will strive to find a mate. The farmer in Antiquity found means by which to get his horse to pull weights. The ancient family used carrot and stick to civilize their young and the ancient kings placed a bounty upon the heads of enemies of the throne. *"Spare the rod and spoil the child"* was a maxim long before the first rat pressed the first bar in the first Skinner box, just as snake-oil cured headaches long before Freud. Aristotle recognized the role of "pleasure" and "pain" in the strengthening of associations; so did Locke and Hume and Mill; and especially so did the nineteenth-century social philosopher Jeremy Bentham, whose *pleasure principle* formed the basis of an entire theory of government. We'll look at these ideas again in the next chapter.

Science often rediscovers (and equally often refutes) the wisdom of the ages and then puts the rediscovery in a form that is more organized, more generalizable—more *lawful.*

One of psychology's first laws, contributed by Thorndike at the end of the last century, is called the *Law of Effect.* Stated most simply, the law asserts that behavior is strengthened or weakened by its effects. Behavior that leads to reward becomes more likely; behavior that leads to punishment becomes less likely. But how are "reward" and "punishment" to be defined? Well, if we are willing to engage in some circularity, we could say that a rewarding stimulus is anything the animal will work to obtain, while a punishing one is anything he will work to avoid or escape.

But we would still need to specify what it is about the stimulus that produces approaching or avoiding behavior. To fill in this gap, psychologists have traditionally taken recourse to biological "explanations." As loyal Darwinians, they have concluded that, at the root of all conceptions of pleasure and pain, some fundamental biological *need* is involved. The need creates an internal "drive" that impels behavior. The behavior ceases only when the drive is reduced; that is, when the biological (cellular) need is eliminated. *Learning* then becomes the process by which behavior leads to *drive reduction.* And, by association, the organism comes to direct attention at those *cues* that signal the availability of reward.

## Peripheralist Theories of Drive

The earliest studies of the biological bases of drives emphasized *peripheral* processes. Hunger, for example, was found to be correlated with the onset of peristaltic contractions of the stomach and intestinal muscles. In some studies of hunger and peristalsis,[5] the experimental subject was required to swallow a deflated balloon; once in the stomach, the balloon was inflated and any pressure exerted on it by stomach contractions recorded. The subject was asked to report when he felt hungry, and gastric contractions or distensions were correlated with these reports. Hunger reliably followed the advent of peristalsis. Even so, as other studies made clear, hunger is not simply the fullness or emptiness of the stomach. When the stomach of an experimental animal is loaded via surgery, thereby producing gastric distension, the animal continues to eat.[6] (Interestingly, if the stomach loading is performed at the time of day when the animals normally eat, they do not eat nearly as much.) Even animals whose stomachs have been surgically removed will continue to eat. Moreover, animals surgically implanted with a cannula in the esophagus (so that what is eaten does not reach the stomach) will stop eating at about that point where, under ordinary circumstances, their stomachs would be full.

Other peripheralist theories focused upon *chemical* cues in the blood. The notion was that hunger is signaled by alterations in blood chemistry, such as lowered blood-sugar levels. Alas, the predictions based upon this idea were never fully realized. Animals fed nonnutritive saccharine, which quickly produces radical reductions in blood-sugar level, behave as if a hearty meal had been consumed. Of course, such data pose little difficulty if one assumes that the animal's eating behavior is to some extent *learned;* that is, the animal comes to associate certain cues (taste, bulk, texture, etc.) with drive reduction, so that even nonnutritive substances—if they have these other properties—can serve as conditioned reinforcers. But once such a learning model is introduced, the biological theory must shift its emphasis from the periphery (viscera, blood, etc.) to the head. Thus, hunger, as a condition leading to behavior, must be sought in brain mechanisms.

## The Hypothalamus and Hunger Drive

Over fifty years ago, clinical reports began appearing which described some interesting facts about a small number of chronically obese patients. Autopsies on these patients revealed tumors in or near a structure known as the *hypothalamus* (shown in Figure 6-4). In the past two decades, neuropsychologists and neurophysiologists have ex-

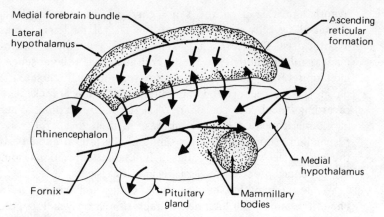

**FIGURE 6-4**
A schematic diagram of the hypothalamus and immediately associated structures. Arrows indicate the direction of information flow. (Adapted from R. A. McCleary and R. Y. Moore, *Subcortical Mechanisms of Behavior: The Psychological Functions of Primitive Parts of the Brain.* New York: Basic Books, 1965.)

plored this structure in a variety of ways and have found it to be an integral part of the biology of hunger and thirst. The most direct evidence comes from studies in which lesions are introduced to specific regions of the hypothalamus. The most important areas thus far localized are the *ventromedial* nucleus and the *lateral* nucleus. (Recall that a *nucleus* is a collection of cell bodies in the central nervous system.)

If the ventromedial nucleus of the hypothalamus is destroyed, the experimental animal (rat, cat, monkey) goes on an eating binge that, before long, results in a doubling of weight. The condition is referred to as hypothalamic *hyperphagia.* Such animals continue to eat about the same number of meals as do normal controls, but their intake per meal is greatly increased. In time, their weight levels off and is maintained at a higher than normal value, although lower than what is attained soon after surgery.

Lesions in the *lateral* hypothalamus produce opposite effects. The animals cease to eat or drink and, if left to themselves, starve to death. The syndrome is called hypothalamic *hypophagia.* If tube feeding is quickly instituted, the animals can be kept alive and eventually resume relatively normal food intake. A rather consistent finding is that normal drinking must return (that is, *adipsia* must be overcome) before normal eating will occur.[7]

Lesions in *both* the ventromedial and the lateral nuclei of the hypothalamus lead to the same condition of hypophagia as that produced by only destruction of the lateral nucleus. It has been hypothesized, therefore, that in the normal animal the ventromedial nucleus *inhibits* activity in the lateral nucleus. In the absence of this inhibition (after destruction of the ventromedial nucleus), hyperphagia ensues because the "appetite center" runs amuck. Single-cell recordings yield data consonant with this interpretation. When units in the ventromedial nucleus increase in their discharge rates, corresponding reductions occur in units of the lateral nucleus. In fact, the two nuclei appear to stand in functional opposition—something like opponent-process mechanisms in color vision.

While the hypothalamic control of eating and drinking behavior is one of the more well-documented facts of neuropsychology, there are still some loose ends. It is known that activity in the ventromedial nucleus is increased when the stomach of an animal is distended with a gastric balloon. Presumably, as the animal fills its stomach by eating, afferent fibers originating in the stomach wall generate impulses that subsequently lead to excitation of units in the ventromedial (appetite-inhibiting) nucleus of the hypothalamus. This finding raises the question of precisely what the hypothalamic cues for eating are. Suppose we argue that the hypothalamic structures really serve as pain centers for the gastric tissues. Filling the stomach leads to the initiation of impulse rates that are aversive; in response to this nociceptive (painful) stimulation, the ventromedial units inhibit further ingestion by acting upon units in the lateral hypothalamus. In the absence of this inhibition, the lateral nucleus simply sustains eating reflexes continuously. Such an interpretation does nothing to vitiate the data but does qualify the use of words such as "hunger," "appetite," and "satiation."

Yet, collectively, the data from studies of gastric distension and contraction, blood chemistry, and hypothalamic activity provide a wholesomely complete picture of the neurobiology of hunger drives. As peripheral deficits (needs) mount, neural impulses in the stomach and intestinal tissues are initiated. Alterations in blood chemistry follow. The stress reactions of the adrenal gland yield an increase in certain hormones, which are known to act specifically on certain regions of the hypothalamus. Thus activated, the lateral hypothalamus may inhibit the ventromedial nucleus while activating those motor areas responsible for eating and drinking. To complete the picture, structures in the hypothalamus or intimately connected to it must respond to changes in environmental temperature because these, too, have effects upon eating. So also do the odor of food, its texture, its taste, the animal's prior experiences with it. Taste has been found to be an especially important variable, at least in the rat. The hypothalamically hyperphagic rat, who under normal circumstances reveals a nearly insatiable need for food, will starve if available food is rendered tasteless. Is the hyperphagic animal, then, simply one that does not habituate to taste, so that each mouthful is as delectable as the one before? If it is *hunger* that the hypothalamus is supposed to be controlling, why should *taste* prove to be such a dominating consideration? Starving men have been known to eat paper to sustain themselves. Finally, if, prior to the introduction of lesions, the experimental animals are made obese or malnourished, the effects of hypothalamic lesions can be reversed; the overnourished "hyperphagic" will fail to eat while the undernourished "hypophagic" will readily eat. This sounds little like a "hunger" center.[8]

### The Hypothalamus and Sexual Drives

Though less well assayed than mechanisms of hunger and thirst, the neural control of sex-related behavior (maternal care, copulation, etc.) has been explored. Again, the hypothalamus turns out to be prominent. If, for example, estrogen (a female hormone) is injected into the hypothalamus of female animals whose ovaries have been removed, they will resume mating behavior—which otherwise does not take place in the ovariectomized animal. Similarly, hormonal injections in the hypothalamus of the male animal can produce *maternal* behavior (nest building, grooming of pups, etc.).[9] Of course, the less dramatic technique of lowering the temperature of the room will also give rise to nest building, so that it is not altogether clear whether these hypothalamic effects are of a "maternal" nature or are rooted in something less exciting.

### The Limbic System and Sexual Drives

More extreme effects upon sexual activity are found in monkeys whose temporal lobes have been removed. One of the earliest studies employing this procedure (bilateral temporal lobectomy) resulted in a series of symptoms known as the *Klüver-Bucy syndrome.* Postoperatively, the monkeys were found to be uncharacteristically tame and also hypersexual. Masturbation, homosexual behavior, and mounting were observed to occur with uncommon frequency. Moreover, the peculiar symptom of *hypermetamorphosis* was in evidence; no matter how frequently an item was placed before a food-deprived animal, he would first place it in his mouth before either eating it or rejecting it. Items included strips of wood, metal, nuts and bolts, and also food. While the animals revealed no basic sensory deficits of a visual nature, they were unable to interpret visual stimuli, at least in terms of edibility. Subsequent studies have indicated that the syndrome occurs because certain structures buried within the medial core of the temporal lobes—specifically, the *amygdala* and the *pyriform cortex*— have been removed, *not* because of the removal of the temporal lobes per se. These structures comprise part of an entire complex of structures referred to collectively as the *limbic system* (see Figure 6-5).

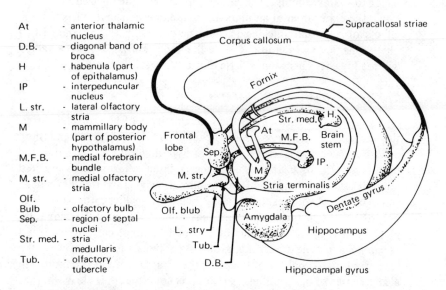

| At | - | anterior thalamic nucleus |
| D.B. | - | diagonal band of broca |
| H | - | habenula (part of epithalamus) |
| IP | - | interpeduncular nucleus |
| L. str. | - | lateral olfactory stria |
| M | - | mammillary body (part of posterior hypothalamus) |
| M.F.B. | - | medial forebrain bundle |
| M. str. | - | medial olfactory stria |
| Olf. Bulb | - | olfactory bulb |
| Sep. | - | region of septal nuclei |
| Str. med. | - | stria medullaris |
| Tub. | - | olfactory tubercle |

**FIGURE 6-5**
Structures of limbic system. Major subcortical structures. Most of these structures have been implicated either in learning, or motivation, or emotion, or memory, in one way or another. Even this simplified sketch is enough to suggest the enormous complexities attending any effort to relate brain structures to psychological functions. (Adapted from P. D. MacLean [1949], Psychosomatic Disease and the "Visceral Brain." Recent Developments Bearing on the Papez Theory of Emotion. *Psychosomatic Medicine, 11,* 338–353.)

Cats with a lesioned pyriform cortex will attempt to mate with kittens, with comitose cats, even with animals of a different species. Female cats with the same lesions are reported to display male sexual behavior patterns (mounting females, exploring the genitalia of females, etc.).

As a last-resort treatment of certain intractable epilepsies or of chronic schizophrenia, surgeons have performed limbic system operations on human patients. These patients, with lesions introduced in areas that produce tameness and hypersexuality in other primates, show few similar postoperative symptoms. The most aggressive manifestation of "hypersexuality" is harmless chatting about "sexual" things or a rather ingenuous hand-holding. To argue that this reduction of affect is due to "self-control" (socialization, shyness, etc.) is to take "sex" out of the limbic system and to replace it with just some mechanical motor elements. That is, if the limbic lesions in man can do no more than get him to hold hands with his nurse, we will have to look beyond the limbic system for the kinds of psychosexual processes that Freud had in mind.

### The Endocrine System and Sexual Drives

The complexity of human sexual behavior is not the only obstacle to a coherent biological theory. At one time, hormonal concentrations (estrogen in the female, androgen in the male) were considered the effective causes of sexual activity. The past decade of research renders any such simple set of substances improbable. Male and female behavior can be triggered by brain stimulation in *either* species, even though the animals have the appropriate sex hormone in their systems. In fact, when castrated male animals are given large doses of *estrogen* (the female hormone), they tend to show increases in *male* sexual behavior.[10] In the absence of proper social rearing, normal sexual behavior does not occur even though there is no abnormality in circulating hormones. And, in humans, even dramatic alterations in hormonal concentration may have little effect upon sexual activity.[11] When pregnant rats are ovariectomized (with the resulting failure to produce estrogen) before their *first* litters, about half of them fail to care for the newborns. Yet the same procedure has nearly no effect on rats that have had previous litters.[12] In other words, there is no direct and simple relationship between hormones and brain activity on the one hand and sexual-parental behavior on the other. The biochemistry is complex; the neurology even more complex; the role of prior experience, age, motivation, and a host of other factors yet to be determined.

## REASONS AND CAUSES: A THEORETICAL AND LOGICAL BIND

When we discussed learning as the outcome of reinforcement and the latter in terms of drive-reduction, we found that we were forced to examine needs, motives, appetites, and the like. The "enlightened machine," we reasoned, must have mechanisms that tend to guarantee survival by triggering or establishing behavior that secures nutrients, avoids tissue damage, and leads to offspring. The role of the hypothalamus in eating and drinking and the role of the other limbic system structures in sexual activity would seem to provide the kind of evidence needed for a neuropsychological theory of motivation. Yet, to say that an animal does $X$ when a particular structure is either stimulated, removed, or destroyed is only to report an observable fact. It is not to provide a theory. The theory is found in our interpretation of the fact. We might say, for instance, that the stimulation is the *cause* of $X$. But that is not the same as saying that the stimulation is the *reason* for $X$.[13] When I turn the ignition key in my car, the *cause* of my actions is to be found in the neuromuscular events that take place in my arm and hand. The *reason,* however, is that I want to drive somewhere. Traditionally, scientists in the mechanistic tradition have eschewed terms such as "want" because of the mentalistic connotations contained therein. After all, "wanting to get somewhere" is learned, and learning is but another neurological outcome. But the matter will not go away so easily. First, we have not yet established that "learning is but another neurological outcome." More significantly, an explanation of how I *learned* to "want" is not the same as an explanation of how I *feel* the want. The problem, in its philosophical form, takes this turn: "If my actions are the result of my *intentions;* and if my intentions are *'mental,'* how can a *'mental'* event have a *physical* consequence? How can a *thesis* move a *muscle?* How can a *hope* fire a *neuron?''* One approach to this problem is to reject dualism (mind-matter distinctions) and assume that, at their base, "wants," "hopes," and "theses" are also physical. But then the obverse issue presents itself: "How can purely material events give rise to mental ones if the latter cannot be described, when they occur, in physical terms?"

Neuropsychological research, there is no doubt, has located some of the important *causal* factors in what, for lack of a more precise term, we have called "motives," "drives," "attention." It has not, however, satisfactorily explained *reasons* or shown that *causes* and *reasons* are but two faces of the same coin. This failure does not seem to be simply the result of semantics. More fundamentally, neuropsychologists have been unable to define and control relevant environmental and behavioral variables. When, for example, connections between the hypothalamus and structures below and above it are severed, the experimental animal is still capable of a startlingly wide range of behavior: he moves about; he even feeds himself, although his food intake is seriously distorted. But does it make any sense to speak of "hunger" in this "preparation," which cannot learn, remember, or engage in any of those behaviors associated with feeling and purpose? Or if we are to speak of "hunger" in such an animal, does it then make any sense to discuss human hunger as a hypothalamic outcome? We know that this "hypothalamic island" that has been created by surgical section is insufficient to allow the animal to integrate environmental and behavioral events. Thus, we conclude that "integration" requires—what?—the remainder of the brain? That being the case, it does little for one seeking explanations to be told about hunger *centers*—unless by "centers" we mean so much of the CNS that the term loses all usefulness.

In our attempt to avoid those conceptual traps that victimized our scientific ancestors, we often adopt a degree of rigor that is laudable but perhaps self-defeating. We avoid assiduously the accusation of anthropomorphism (attributing human characteristics to nonhuman animals). But in adopting this antianthropomorphic stance, we may actually overcompensate to the point of refusing to attribute human characteristics to human animals. Moreover, since we have agreed to study nonhuman forms in an attempt to understand human life, we have, *de facto,* permitted anthropomorphism to enter the dialogue. If I have no reluctance to discuss the hypothalamus of the rat as a "hunger" center, why should I shrink back from the notion that the rat *feels* hungry as I myself do? And if I am willing to share this feeling with the rat, then, in my attempt to understand *hunger,* I must do more than just examine *eating behavior.* The latter may (or may not) follow the former, but it surely *is* not the former. In other words, I must be willing to discuss and attempt to study the *emotions.*

## NOTES AND REFERENCES

1. The classical demonstration of this relationship was provided by G. Moruzzi and H. Magoun: *Electroencephalog. clin. Neurophysiol.,* 1949, *1,* 455–473.
2. For an excellent review, see D. B. Lindsley (pp.1553–1593) in Field, Magoun, & Hall (Eds.), *Handbook of Physiology, Neurophysiology III,* Washington, D. C.: (American Physiological Society, 1960).
3. See, for example, R. Hernandez-Peon, H. Scherrer, & M. Jouvet: *Science,* 1956, *123,* 331–332.
4. These and related effects are discussed by P. B. Bradley in his chapter (pp. 338–344) in de Reuk and Knight (Eds.), *Animal Behavior and Drug Action* (Boston: Little, Brown & Co., 1964).
5. See, for example, W. B. Cannon & A. L. Washburn: *Am. J. Physiol.,* 1912, *29,* 441–454.

6. See, for a recent reawakening of the matter, Quartermain et al.: *Science*, 1971, *173*, 941.

7. For a thorough review of the literature on the hypothalamus and appetitive behavior, consult P. Teitelbaum and A. N. Epstein: *Psychol. Rev.*, 1962, 74–90.

8. See, for example, Keesey, *J. comp. physiol. Psychol.*, 1970. Also, against the view of a hunger "center" it should be pointed out that, with a welter of techniques, the following areas have all been implicated in either eating or drinking or both: hippocampus, mamillary body, thalamus, cingulate gyrus, septum, fornix, amygdala, and ventral tegmentum. The reader might consult J. N. Coury: *Science*, 1967, *156*, 1763–1765; also, W. Wyricka & R. Doty: *Exp. Brain Res.*, 1966, *1*, 152–160.

9. A. E. Fisher: *Science*, 1965, *124*, 228–229.

10. H. H. Feder & R. E. Whelan: *Science*, 1965, *147*, 306–307.

11. J. Money (pp. 1383–1400), in W. C. Young (Ed.), *Sex and Internal Secretions* (Baltimore: Williams & Wilkins, 1961).

12. H. Molz & E. Wiener: *J. comp. physiol. Psychol.*, 1966, *62*, 382–387.

13. Distinctions between "reasons" and "causes" have been discussed in philosophy since Aristotle. The issue was raised in modern times by, among others, Wittgenstein in his *Blue Book*. My own distinction, which I believe to be different from those made by others, is that causes refer to mechanisms and reasons do not *necessarily*. The matter is raised again in the last chapter. Note, however, that reasons and causes follow a different logic. Causes and effects are related by entailment in that the very concept of an "effect" entails some antecedent cause. Thus, given a cause, the effect inescapably follows. Given a reason, however, we are not faultless in predicting immediately subsequent actions. One may have every reason to do something and yet not do it. For example, one may have every reason to wish for immortality, but nothing follows from this by way of action. Similarly, we have good reasons for desiring a just world, but the rational analysis at the root of concepts of justice does not necessarily become translated into action of any kind.

# 7
# Twin Masters: Pleasure and Pain

In his *Principles of Morals and Legislation,* the nineteenth-century utilitarian Jeremy Bentham proclaimed, "The business of government is to promote the happiness of society by rewarding and punishing." He argued that nature had placed man "under the governance of two masters": *pleasure* and *pain.* It was on this man's lap that young John Stuart Mill received his earliest instruction in political theory. Bentham's corpse still attracts visitors to the London School of Economics. Most important, his "pleasure principle" continues to be the authoritative foundation of all arguments that begin with the assumption that the last criterion of legitimacy is happiness. The whole fabric of *behaviorism,* Thorndike's law of effect, drive-reduction theories of learning, Freud's *id,* Skinner's *Walden Two*—virtually all empirically based psychological principles spring from Bentham's twin masters, pleasure and pain.

Of course, the notion did not originate with Bentham. Even the caveman probably civilized his litter with a stick, and antiquity is rife with illustrations of punishment as an instrument of control. In formal philosophical language, John Locke respected the role of pleasure and pain in cementing our associations, and David Hume insisted that even philosophers are guided chiefly by hedonistic considerations. Then, shortly after the half-way point in the nineteenth century, Charles Darwin put the great seal of science on the matter by defining the purpose of creation as *survival.* To us, this all makes perfectly good sense. After a sustained epoch of war and technology, we have little difficulty accepting the merits of a pragmatic ethic. Our ancestors, however, had a tougher time with such ideas. They were conditioned by seventeenth- and eighteenth-century philosophers who sought "higher" laws and more noble purposes. The great French *philosophes* (Voltaire, Diderot, d'Alembert) would have had little patience with Bentham's practical politics. Even Thomas Jefferson, a devout liberal, looked upon political freedom as an inalienable right, not simply as something that makes man *happy*. Bentham reversed the order of the argument; it makes us happy and therefore it is right.

The bridge from these issues to neuropsychology is short. We cross it with the contention that if man is capable of pleasure and pain there must be a neural mechanism involved. In other words, we address ourselves to the biological bases of emotion.

But what is emotion? What, for instance, is *fear?* Suppose we are asked to determine whether a kitten is afraid of a particular object—say, a magnet. How will we proceed to make this determination? We will probably begin by putting the magnet in the vicinity of the kitten. Suppose that the kitten retreats whenever the magnet is brought near; in fact, even when deprived of food, he will not approach a food tray if the magnet is on the tray. We might feel safe in concluding that indeed the kitten is afraid of magnets. Now let us try to determine whether a toy soldier is afraid of magnets. Each time we bring the magnet (its South Pole) toward the toy, which rests on wheels, the toy rolls backward. From our experience with the kitten, are we now to conclude that the toy is also afraid of magnets? If not, then how are we to judge emotion in any object, living or otherwise? This is the central dilemma in all studies of "emotionality" in nonverbal organisms. The only dependent variable that can be used is *behavior,* and there is simply no logical basis upon which to rest the assertion that behavior is or even reflects *feeling.* Even with man, who can *say* that he is "happy" or "frightened" or "angry"; it is an act of faith on our part when we believe him. We know from our personal experience that we have these feelings and that we describe them the way our subject does. We conclude, therefore, that he, too, must have these feelings. But we have no way of proving—by experiment or by logical argument—that he has such feelings or that, if he does, they are the same as ours when we use the same words. Again we confront the distinction between *causes* and *reasons*. We observe a sprinter poised under the gun. A shot is fired, and the sprinter takes off with all deliberate speed down the cinder track. Is he avoiding the gun? Is he afraid of the gun? Is the shot the reason for his running? Of course not. The reason for his running is that he is engaged in a race, which he cannot win if he starts to run before the shot is fired. In this respect, the shot is the *cause* of his running (not the proximate cause, which is neuromuscular, but the first in a chain of causes). The race is the reason. If we ask him later why he ran down the track, he will surely not say that he did so because of the shot. Now, instead of using a pistol shot, let's put ethical issues aside and implant electrodes in our sprinter's auditory nerve. Again, he is poised at the start line, and now we deliver an electrical stimulus to the nerve. Off he goes. Is the electrical stimulus the reason for his running? Not at all. The same stimulus delivered later that night, when our track star is having dinner, will not result in his romping across the table. Instead, he will report that he is hearing something that sounds like a shot. Again, the *reason* for his running is the race.[1] Getting back to ethics, let us this time place an electrode in the posterior hypothalamus of a cat. We deliver a pulse and observe the animal to hiss, spit, extend its claws, and strike out at a doll dropped into his cage. Is the cat in a state of rage? Is the stimulation of hypothalamus the reason? We will get back to this issue again. First, let us consider various theories concerning the biological bases of emotion.

## PERIPHERALIST THEORIES OF EMOTIONS

As with biological theories of drives and motives, the earliest theories of the emotions attributed their existence to *peripheral* events. The most prominent of these theories was that advanced by William James and C. G. Lange. According to the James-Lange hypothesis, a rewarding or punishing stimulus activates those mechanisms that control the actions of the *autonomic nervous system* (see Figure 3-4)—actions such as changes in pulse, heart rate, respiration rate, blood-adrenalin concentration, gastric musculature, pupillary response, peripheral blood flow, muscle tension, skin resistance. The *sympathetic* branch of the autonomic nervous system, largely by its action on the adrenal glands, produces alarm or arousal effects; the *parasympathetic* branch has very nearly opposite effects. According to the James-Lange view, a *felt* emotion is but the consequence of these peripheral changes: "You see a bear, you run, and *then* you become frightened." In other words, the stimulus (a bear) activates the sympathetic branch of the autonomic nervous system, thereby altering myriad biological (visceral) events; the *sum* of these visceral changes *is* the emotion of fear.

The deficiencies of this view were recognized early and underscored experimentally. First, recordable changes in various physiological responses, such as those cited above, do not correlate highly with reported feelings. Put briefly, all intense emotional states (whether fear, rage, sexual excitement, or unrestrained laughter) are accompanied by comparable changes in peripheral physiology. Furthermore, animals subjected to complete (surgical) removal of the capacity for external stimulation still manifest "emotional" behavior. Finally, human subjects are very poor at recognizing changes in their own autonomic activity, an ability that would be necessary if such changes were to be the cues (causes) responsible for emotional experiences. The fact is that the kind of effect a given autonomic agent (e.g., epinephrine) has upon the feelings of an individual is determined by a host of factors, including especially the individual's perception of the context in which such agents are administered. In a representative study[2] one group of subjects were given epinephrine and told truthfully what the likely physiological effects would be: some light-headedness, rapid pulse, feelings of excitement. Another group received the same drug but were misinformed about the effects. Each subject was then exposed to a "stooge," who attempted to enlist the subject in a series of silly tasks, such as playing basketball with a roll of paper. The individuals who had been instructed accurately and truthfully were immune to the euphoric atmosphere created by the stooge. Those who did not know the true effects of the drug were easily engaged in frivolous activities. Thus, the drug effects were finally determined not simply by their biological consequences but also by complex perceptual factors.

## CENTRAL MECHANISMS FOR EMOTIONS: THE LIMBIC SYSTEM

The inability of peripheral mechanisms to account for the facts of emotional experience drew attention to *central* mechanisms. The earliest investigators performed ablations in order to try to determine those structures essential to displays of "emotional" behavior. The early findings were suggestive but inconclusive.[3] Removal of the entire cortical mantle still permitted animals (cats) to display "rage," but the rage was irrelevantly directed; the animal would attack in the direction in which he was pointed rather than at the location of the noxious stimulus. The Klüver-Bucy syndrome (discussed in Chapter 6) was discovered in monkeys after bilateral removal of the temporal cortex. One of the most reliable effects of this ablation is the docility it produces. This effect on "emotion" strongly implicated those structures located *within* the core of the temporal lobes as well as those placed more medially. Recall that these structures form the *limbic system* (see Figure 6-6). It is within this system that diseases associated with hyperemotionality in man are sometimes found. It is here that modern neuropsychology attempts to locate the basis of feelings.

The existence of an "emotion system" in the brain was first proposed by the anatomist J. W. Papez .[4] Papez based his ideas on only a small set of clinical findings; yet, within the restraints imposed upon any biological theory of emotion, he has proved to be remarkably accurate. The now-famous *Papez circuit* begins with the hippocampus and successively incorporates the fornix, the mammillary bodies, the mammilo-thalamic pathways, the septum, the anterior thalamus, and, from the thalamus, projections that finally involve the cingulate cortex. Here is our "Freudian" brain and even in the names of its parts we sense deep mystery and foreboding drama. "Hippocampus"—it has the ring of an ancient general waging fiercely against numberless forces. "Mammilo-thalamic"—like some primitive incantation uttered to call up spirits of doubtful honor. And, as brains go, these are among the very oldest organs in the evolution of the animal kingdom. The ageless reptile, with only a meager cortical endowment, possesses a defiantly elaborate limbic system. In the primates, it sits below the cortex. By location, by age, and by function it appears ideally suited to bring feeling to bear upon reason. What happens when we disturb the monster? Well, as usual, that depends.

The original classification of limbic structures has undergone some revision. In addition to those cited above, current workers usually include the amygdala and portions of the hypothalamus. The principal techniques employed in studies of the limbic system are ablation and (with growing frequency) electrical stimulation. Many species (including our own) have been studied, although the literature is dominated by research employing rats, cats, and monkeys. To date, the studies have been limited to descriptions of gross behavior patterns associated with "rage," "fear," and "anxiety." Where human subjects have been used, introspective reports of "feelings" have also been recorded.

### "AGGRESSION"

Many studies have been conducted in which "rage" and "aggression" have followed stimulation of various regions of the limbic system and the brain stem. The most reliable effects have been obtained from stimulation of the posterior portions of the hypothalamus, the mid-hypothalamus, the amygdala, and, outside the limbic system, various regions of the neocortex. The behavior produced by electrical stimulation is usually complex and of a duration equal to or longer than the period of stimulation. Cats hiss, claw (often at imaginary objects), bare their teeth, spit, and hunch their backs. Their fur stands high, tails swish, and posture menaces. Monkeys grimace, vocalize loudly, bare their teeth, and strike out at objects placed before them, including hands. When ablations are performed, a directed constellation of "aggressive" responses requires the sparing of the posterior third of the hypothalamus. That is, even when massive areas of the cortex and the diencephalon have been removed, the animal can still offer an integrated pattern of "ferocious" behaviors if the posterior hypothalamus is intact.[5] Typically, the "rage threshold" is lowered in that even the mildest tactile stimulation will trigger the full complement of responses.

Taking a more elementaristic approach, certain investigators have attempted to remove, item by item, various components of "aggression." For example, they have located by stimulation a region that gives rise to hissing. This region is then ablated, and a hypothalamic region which normally produces "rage" is stimulated. With the other structure removed, all of the "rage" components *except hissing* occur.

Interpreting the results of studies in this area has proved to be more difficult than obtaining them. It is not clear, for example, what is being stimulated when the stimulation method is employed. The "aggressive" behavior may be the result of *pain* produced by the electrical stimulus. That is, rather than finding the locus of "aggression," investigators may simply have found areas which, when stimulated, give rise to noxious internal sensations to which the animal responds "aggressively." This appears likely in those studies reporting a significant lowering of "rage" thresholds. Normal cats, when gently stroked, tend not to initiate a series of destructive behaviors. That "hypothalamic" cats do makes one wonder just what the stimulus to the hypothalamus is achieving. There is the added problem of the incomparability of data obtained from stimulation studies and those obtained from ablation studies. It has been found, for example, that structure $X$, which when stimulated leads to "rage," also leads to rage when removed. Similarly, the effects of stimulation are sometimes the same as the effects of introducing a lesion in the same area. Equally perplexing is the finding that opposite patterns of behavior are produced when the same structure is stimulated with currents of different intensity. Great differences are also obtained when animals of different ages or with different reinforcement histories are used. Thus, the alley cat and the laboratory cat may respond in entirely different ways.[6] Such differences have been incompletely explored. There is a disappointingly thin literature concerned with genetic and early-experience variables as they relate to the effects of brain stimulation. A small but growing literature in *comparative* psychology gives one cause for some concern in that different species react very differently to stimulation of the "same" (anatomically the same) structures. If the rat can't help us understand the rabbit, is it likely that the monkey will inform the man?

While we must always respect the distinction between causes and reasons, we can suspend our skepticism momentarily and accept the assertion that "aggression," no matter how we define it, reveals itself in behavior as a result of the activity of the nervous system. This generalization is as valid as it is trivial. Why, then, should experiments lead to such diverse and contradictory findings? We can begin to answer this question by adopting the posture of fashionable Darwinists. To survive, animals must be able to attack, to defend, and to flee. The animal that runs from his own food supply will not be around long enough to breed similarly inclined progeny. Nor will the mouse that challenges the lion. To one or another extent, all species probably have stimulus-specific sensory apparatus (such as the "bug detectors" of frogs or the cortical cells in the visual system of cats). That is, on the basis of millennia of selection pressures, existing forms of animal life must be equipped to respond in rather stereotyped fashion to stimuli possessing physical characteristics relevant to survival. Of course, evolution brings with it greater and greater independence of action. As the capacity to learn and remember grows, the need for reliance upon reflexive movements wanes. Thus, what we discover to be inevitabilities lower in phylogeny may simply be tendencies among more advanced forms. How does an inevitability become transformed into a tendency? Probably by *inhibition*. In a very real sense, learning is the ability to control reflexes, to inhibit otherwise rigid stimulus-response chains. This control is acquired through experience. It should not surprise us, therefore, that animals as advanced as rats, cats, and monkeys should display great individual differences in stimulation and ablation studies. With monkeys, who usually have a defined hierarchy that determines the social behavior of each member in the colony, we would expect the animals on the top and the bottom rungs to respond differently to limbic system stimulation. We would also expect age differences, differences due to handling, differences due to prior learning. Even in the rat such subtleties must prevail. We can train (condition) a rat to "fear" (i.e., unfailingly avoid) a neutral object such as a rubber doll. If this rat is then hypothalamically stimulated, will he attack the doll? We can also breed rats for conditionability in such avoidance-learning situations. Does the strain that learns to avoid most quickly also attack least frequently when hypothalamically stimulated? In other words, can we systematically explore genetic and experiential factors in order to predict more unequivocally the consequences of brain stimulation? Until such studies come to dominate the literature, we can say only that some animals do $X$ some of the time when stimulated in some areas with a current of so many milliamperes—but not always and not all animals, etc., etc.

## "FEAR"

The toy soldier who shuns the magnet is a model of "fear" research in neuropsychology. In these studies, electrodes are chronically implanted in an animal; the animal is then placed in a cage and observed as different objects are placed nearby. When a certain area of the limbic system is stimulated, a cat, for example, will arch away from the very same mouse that he would ordinarily devour. But stimulation at another location renders the cat "fearless." Here, the cat is first conditioned to avoid a light; that is, when the light is flashed, the cat must leap over a barrier in order to avoid shock. Presumably, the consequence of this conditioning is to create "fear" or "anxiety" in the face of the conditioned stimulus. However, with appropriate stimulation, the avoidance behavior disappears. Ablation of portions of the cingulate cortex produces such "fearlessness," a finding that encouraged the use of this operation on human patients suffering from chronic anxiety. Postoperatively, some patients report reduced anxiety, but the effects are neither consistent nor clear-cut.

## "PLEASURE CENTERS"

Some researchers have investigated the effects of self-administered intracranial shock (ICS). In such studies, electrodes are placed at any one of a number of locations (the median forebrain bundle, hypothalamus, amygdala, portions of the hippocampus, etc.); when the animal presses a lever, a brief shock is delivered to the structure. Experimental animals sit for hours and continue to stimulate themselves at incredibly high rates—as much as 100 times per minute[7]—stopping only when exhausted. The animals will cross an electrically charged field in order to gain access to the lever. They will speed down a runway, traverse a lake, overcome painful obstacles in order to obtain this shock. Even when starved, they will choose this lever instead of one that leads to food. Human patients, with electrodes in analogous areas, report sensations of giddiness, drunkenness, and euphoria when stimulation is applied. Is it here that Bentham's masters reside?

Unfortunately, it is not clear that these centers are pleasure-producing or even reward-producing, at least in the way that rewards usually come to control behavior. The hungry animal who presses a bar associated with the delivery of food behaves quite differently in the ICS setting. He continues insatiably to stimulate himself; yet, unlike the normal animal, he extinguishes almost with the first nonreinforced trial. His "interest" in the bar is engaged only as long as it pays off. For this reason, it is difficult, if not impossible, to establish the kind of behavior associated with partial (ratio) reinforcement. Moreover, with few exceptions, animals cannot be trained to learn complex behavioral chains in order to obtain ICS. That is, the range of *learning* is seriously constricted when the reinforcer is ICS. Extinction appears with sudden rapidity and vanishes with nearly equal speed—nothing like the gradual extinction that attends nonreinforcement with food or water. To get the ICS animal to behave in a way that looks anything like what we get with food or liquid deprivation, it is usually necessary to couple ICS with these very same deprivation procedures. Thus, why the animals persevere in pressing the ICS bar is not presently known. What is clear is that ICS—whatever its effects may be—is neither a primary nor a secondary reinforcer as these terms are conventionally employed in behavioral psychology.

What the results of ICS research boil down to is this: An animal capable of delivering shocks to certain brain regions does not extinguish as long as the stimulus reliably follows the response. Such an observation would seem to imply pathology more than a simulation of normal reinforcement operations. In truth, the animals' behaviors remind one more of the "hypermetamorphosis" of the Klüver-Bucy syndrome. The ICS animal perseveres similarly, unable to relate the *neural* properties of stimulation to the balance of his physiological condition; that is, he seems to suffer from a kind of *interoceptive agnosia*. At least intuitively, we reject the idea that nuts and bolts are reinforcing to the Klüver-Bucy animal. By what logic, then, do we defend the proposition that ICS is reinforcing to the ICS animal? Before we conclude that we have found the "centers" of hedonism, we must try to determine more rigorously what ICS is doing to the animal. This determination will require more complex experimental designs than are now common in this field. For example, if ICS has its effects by reducing "anxiety," we should be able to condition "anxiety" (tone followed ten seconds later by shock will lead to conditioned increases in heart rate, peripheral vasoconstriction, changes in blood-adrenalin concentration, and many other peripheral correlates of "anxiety"). These changes will develop during the ten-second "anticipation" interval. Will ICS during this interval preclude the development of those visceral events associated with "anxiety"? These, after all, are what we usually mean when we discuss biological "causes" of emotional states. Although we can never know how a monkey "feels," we do know that certain conditions give rise to reports of anxiety in people; these conditions are correlated with visceral changes that can be induced in other animals by the same procedures.

Research of this kind will not necessarily answer the "philosophical" questions. For example, even if we could demonstrate that the visceral correlates of anxiety are attenuated or eliminated by stimulation of particular brain sites, we still could not speak confidently of "pleasure centers" or "euphoria centers." Few would contest the notion that visceral correlates of anxiety are under biological control. That the controlling mechanisms are ultimately traceable to structures in the limbic system is interesting but irrelevant to the question "What are the physical determinants of anxiety?" Anxiety is our *reflection upon* biological events and not the events themselves. Consequently, even if we induced all the ordinary correlates of anxiety (increased heart rate and respiration, increased adrenalin concentration, heightened blood pressure, and other visceral events) in a patient in coma, we could not assert that we had created "anxiety." The emotion is not the physical occurrence but a *knowledge* of the occurrence.

A failure to appreciate this distinction is partially responsible for the confusion that attends discussions of "machine intelligence." The confusion centers on the tendency to argue whether or not a machine "knows" *X, Y,* and *Z.* Stated this way, there really is no issue. Quite clearly, if I strike a button on which is inscribed 7, another with the symbol +, and a third displaying 5 and then press a master button reading "SUM" and the machine prints out 12, I must fairly conclude that the machine *knows* how to add. In the same sense, electrical wiring in an office *knows* Ohm's law, and the pressure cooker on the stove *knows* Boyle's. However, in none of these instances can the system be said *to know that it knows.* In order to know that it knows, it must be able to compare its present state of knowledge with a state in which that knowledge was not present. That is, knowledge of knowledge presumes prior ignorance; and there was not a time when the laws of Boyle or Ohm were *not known* by the respective devices. Indeed, it is in the nature of a physical law that its validity is independent of any awareness of it. This is not to say that the pressure cooker and the electrical circuit are *necessarily* non-conscious. Nor is it to aver that the adding machine does not know that it knows the solution to the addition problem. It is only to say that the existence of consciousness (a knowledge of knowledge) cannot be verified through a demonstration of knowledge. Thus, to the question "Does the machine know $X, Y, Z$?" we must answer "yes" if the machine is capable of providing $X$ or $Y$ or $Z$ when interrogated. But we cannot apply this same criterion to the question "Does the machine know that it knows $X, Y, Z$?" For, even if it fails to provide $X$ or $Y$ or $Z$, we still have to accept the possibility that it knows that it *doesn't* know or that it knows but refuses to answer or that it knows it knows but its response mechanisms are in disrepair. In short, the expression of knowledge is not necessarily a state of awareness. Similarly, the display of "emotional" behavior does not necessarily imply a state of emotionality.

## RESEARCH WITH HUMAN PATIENTS

Any statement concerning *emotion* must finally seek its validity in studies of man. But when man is the subject of studies concerned with brain mechanisms and emotion, confusing results are obtained. First of all, only patients with long-standing diseases that have not responded to more modest forms of therapy have been examined. Second, the brain is a very big world, and electrodes can explore only its smallest villages. Third, the subjective reports of patients who have been institutionalized for their unconventionality are regrettably more suspect than verbal reports usually and justifiably are. We all know from our private experiences that words are often not nearly sufficient to describe feelings. Nor have we methods of determining whether the same words mean the same thing even when used by the same person at different times, let alone by different people. Finally, feelings are determined *contextually;* they are in response *to* something. The "something" is interpreted; it is perceived; it is perceived in the light of experience, often the experiences of a lifetime. A man flat on his back in the operating room receiving pulses to his amygdala and asked "Now how do you feel?" is not ideally suited to reveal the spectrum of human emotion. Well, how *does* he feel? Usually he feels quite relaxed when certain areas of the limbic system are being stimulated. As with the prefrontally lobotomized patient, he is less disturbed by his condition, less affected by those concerns of which he is still aware. He may also experience an inexplicable giddiness leading to bursts of laughter. In the field of "psychosurgery," whose literature is growing at an alarming rate, we find patients with a history of violent flare-ups made docile, patients with chronic anxiety made casual, patients with long-term psychopathological withdrawal made more outgoing. And yet we find little that is similar to the results of subhuman research. The uncontrollable "rage" of the hypothalamic cat has not been witnessed in the human patient, nor has the paralyzing fear, the blind aggression, the mindless escape.[8] What we do discover are rather mild shifts in affect, confusing but often relieving "sensations," nothing to rave about but interesting.[9]

## THE PROBLEM OF DEFINITIONS

We began our discussion with the question of *where* in the CNS the emotions are to be found. Clearly, our failure to answer that question is based in part upon our inability to define *what* we are looking for. Surely we are looking for more than those centers which, when stimulated, lead to hissing, spitting, scratching, and biting. Presumably, we could find motor areas that lead to such behaviors even if all sensory areas were destroyed. No doubt, those skillfull in such matters and with the time to devote could isolate a tiny piece of motor cortex which, when activated, would result in the extension of a cat's claws. Is this aggression? Is it an aggression "center"? More conservatively, is it the nail-extension center? Well, if it is, the finding is not very interesting. After all, we all agreed in advance that if cats can extend their claws they must have a mechanisms that allows it. But why does the cat do this when a mouse runs by? Once we admit "why" into the discourse, we are seeking *reasons*. Alas, nobody knows why the cat claws the mouse. And to claim that we can in any case make him stop by stimulating a brain center is almost trite. We can do the same thing by cutting his foot off or, more humanely, by removing the mouse.

When we try to define "emotion," we realize at once that we are using one word for a great assortment of conditions. Our feelings vary in quality, in intensity, in duration. Experimentally, the conditions we employ to create "fear" or "anxiety" just don't come close to those events in life that cripple our actions and distort our aims. And when we enter the world to study real-life victims of fear, they are usually so wracked by the consequences of their condition that generalizing anything we discover in them to healthy people is hazardous. Many patients who get to the operating room because of chronic psychiatric disturbances are found to be suffering from lesions in the brain. We might wish to conclude that *all* such disturbances are the result of pathology but that the condition often remains undetected. But then we confront the onus of defining "disturbance." Psychiatric disorders come in every shade and variation, and what is "normal" is often a tentative and situational commodity. Everyone has some limit beyond which his behavior gets away from him. For some, the limit is low;

and, if the climate is right, they will break. It isn't likely that the "break" awaits a lesion. Most of us die quietly and are put to rest long before the eager pathologist or medical student even knows we're gone. Thus, only a vanishingly small fraction of the world's population ever enjoys the attention of an autopsy. Most of us may pass on with something alien in our heads; after all, we must die of something. The neurological deficits found in many psychiatric patients may however be the only normal thing about them.

## A SUMMARY AND METAPHOR

Science in the modern world has some of the same characteristics as Natural Philosophy in the ancient world. It is bold, confident, skeptical, and eager for converts. To keep it on the straight and narrow, a discipline needs critics, loving critics. One of the best in antiquity was Aristophanes. While respecting the aims and efforts of the philosophers, he recognized a certain lack of restraint in their optimism, a certain lack of subtlety in their phrasing of explanations. He was an intelligent and cultivated man, quite aware of the difference between "naming" and "explaining," between causes and correlations. In his play *Clouds* he describes the plight of Strepsiades, who is bitter over his failure to understand the meaning of life. Believing that he has been deceived by the half-truths and corruptions of reason perpetrated by his schooling, he enlists in Socrates' school, hoping that the philosopher will set him aright. In his first encounter with the great thinker, he is chided for his religious beliefs:

STREPSIADES: But by the Earth! is our father, Zeus, the Olympian, not a god?

SOCRATES: Zeus! what Zeus! Are you mad? There is no Zeus.

STREPSIADES: What are you saying now? Who causes the rain to fall? Answer me that!

SOCRATES: Why, these, and I will prove it. Have you ever seen it raining without clouds? Let Zeus then cause rain with a clear sky and without their presence!

STREPSIADES: By Apollo! that is powerfully argued! For my own part I always thought it was Zeus urinating into a sieve. But tell me, who is it makes the thunder, which I so much dread?

SOCRATES: These (clouds) when they roll over one another.

STREPSIADES: But how can that be, you most daring among men?

SOCRATES: Being full of water, and forced to move along, they are of necessity precipitated in rain, being fully distended with moisture from the regions where they have been floating; hence, they bump each other heavily and burst with great noise.

STREPSIADES: But is it not Zeus who forces them to move?

SOCRATES: Not at all; it's the aerial Whirlwind.

STREPSIADES: The Whirlwind! ah! I did not know that. So Zeus, it seems, has no existence, and it's the Whirlwind that reigns in his stead? But you have not told me yet what makes the roll of the thunder? . . . .

SOCRATES: Take yourself as an example. When you have heartily gorged on stew at the Panathenaea, you get throes of stomach-ache and then suddenly your belly resounds with prolonged rumbling.

STREPSIADES: Yes, yes, by Apollo! I suffer, I get colic, then the stew sets to rumbling like thunder and finally bursts forth with a terrific noise. At first it's but a little gurgling *pappax, pappax!* then it increases, *papapappax.* . . .

Later, Strepsiades meets his son and is eager to show off his recently acquired knowledge. His son, Phidippides, has little patience with the old man but for the moment is willing to converse:

STREPSIADES: Oh! you fool! to believe in Zeus at your age!

PHIDIPPIDES: What is there in that to make you laugh?

STREPSIADES: You are then a tiny child, if you credit such anti-quated rubbish! But come here, that I may teach you; I will tell you something very necessary to know to be a man; but do not repeat it to anybody.

PHIDIPPIDES: Tell me, what is it?

STREPSIADES: Just now you swore by Zeus.

PHIDIPPIDES: Sure I did.

STREPSIADES: Do you see how good it is to learn? Phidippides, there is no Zeus.

PHIDIPPIDES: What is there then?

STREPSIADES: The Whirlwind has driven out Zeus and is King now.

PHIDIPPIDES: What drivel!

For more than a century, psychology has attempted to explain the emotions scientifically. It has employed verbal report, conditioning, gross recordings of certain physiological processes. Unable to reach a comprehensive understanding of the emotions with these techniques, some decided to examine more basic physiological processes. The upshot of this work has been the discovery of "emotion centers." Has the Whirlwind replaced Zeus?

## NOTES AND REFERENCES

1. In formal terms, it may be argued that "reasons" refer to *a priori* considerations while "causes" refer only *a posteriori*. This is in accord with the present thesis, which treats causes as necessarily implying a mechanism or physical agency or agency ultimately reducible to physical events. Thus, from the sprinter's running we must adduce an antecedent cause; e.g., neural excitation of the musculature of the legs. Accordingly, given a cause, there must be a consequence. However, the existence of a reason does not *necessarily* imply an outcome of any sort. In his seminal paper *Actions, Reasons, and Causes* (*J. Philosophy*, LX, 1963), Donald Davidson argues that a reason consists in the agent's positive attitude toward a particular outcome and his belief that a given action will produce it. According to this definition, "the primary reason for an action is its cause." If I understand the sense in which he states, "Primary reasons consist of attitudes and beliefs, which are states or dispositions, not events; therefore they cannot be causes," then his position and my own are not far apart. In the present context, the sprinter's *belief* that by running he might win the race is a state or disposition. It is not the *cause* of his running. The latter has more to do with the starter's pistol shot than it has to do with the sprinter's belief. Indeed, a sprinter might become paralyzed and still believe that if he were to run he might win the race. In this instance, the *causes* of running have been removed while the reasons persist. Davidson later contends that mental events are causes, but, at this point, we part. If they are "causes," it is in their ability to influence the more immediate *neural* causes. Mental "dispositions" do not necessarily lead to actions, but neuromuscular events do. Perhaps this is Davidson's view also, as when he concludes, "Some causes have no agents. Primary among these are those states and changes of state in persons which, because they are reasons as well as causes, make persons voluntary agents."

2. S. Schachter & J. Singer: *Psychol. Rev.*, 1962, *69*, 379-399.

3. P. Bard: *Am. J. Physiol.*, 1928, *84*, 490-515.

4. J. W. Papez: *Arch. neurol. Psychiat.*, 1937, *38*, 725-743.

5. P. Bard, op. cit.; Also, W. R. Ingram: *Electroencephalog. clin. Neurophysiol.*, 1952, *4*, 397-406.

6. e.g., H. Ursin: *Exp. Neurol.*, 1965, *11*, 64-79.

7. J. Olds: *Science,* 1958, *127,* 315–323.
8. There are some apparent exceptions. For example, see H. E. King (pp. 477–486) in D. E. Sheer (Ed.), *Electrical Stimulation of the Brain* (Austin: Univ. Texas Press, 1961). One of King's patients, under amygdaloid stimulation, expressed intense anger.
9. Ethical issues raised by "psychosurgery" are discussed by D. N. Robinson, *American Psychologist,* 1973 (February).

# 8
# Language, Universals, and the Limits of Knowledge

Benjamin Whorf, the outstanding linguist, described language as *"the best show man puts on,"* as if to acknowledge that only whimsy can convey the mystery and centrality of language, our most precious achievement.

There have been long debates on exactly what language is. Is it merely speech or communication? Do other species have it, albeit in simpler form? Is it acquired as just another form of behavior? Is it innate? Does the parrot display it when he utters, "Polly wanna cracker"? Is the dog announcing his fury with a bark or the cat with a hiss? Is the baby's "goo" the first primitive expression of linguistic form?[1]

When the honey bee returns to the hive, it engages in a "dance," the pattern of which can be used by other bees to locate where the dancing bee has just been. Thus, a symbolic representation of space has been communicated by one organism, and this received information can be used by others to solve a problem. Shall we admit this behavior into the domain of "language"? Clearly, we must if we define language as symbolic communication that allows the passage of information from a sender to a receiver. The hungry baby who cries for food satisfies the same definition. So does the puppy who learns to give us his paw. Indeed, the clouds reliably report their supersaturation by raining. It should be getting clear that something is wrong with our definition. It does not eliminate those events that we all believe have no place in a discussion of language. We might be willing to call the "dancing" bee or even the puppy a linguist. But clouds?

The clouds do inform us of impending rain, and when they take on a certain texture and mass, they tell us to find shelter. We reject the clouds' communication as language because, we insist, the clouds do not *know* what they are telling us; they do not *intend* to inform us. But how do we know that the baby intends to inform? Or the puppy? For that matter, as I type these lines, how does anyone other than myself *know* what or even if I intend? In order to eliminate the clouds, we must invoke the concept of *intention* in our definition of language; and once we have taken this reassuring step, the whole matter becomes one of personal speculation.

There is one thing that babies, puppies, parrots, and clouds have in common: *They cannot lie.* The ability to lie may be a rather cynical criterion of language, but it does convey a very subtle character of language: Its structure is lawful, but its content need not be. Within the marginal constraints imposed by rules of grammar, anything goes. This is not the case with our other illustrations. Clouds and puppies and babies are too truthful; or, if you like, too perfect. Moreover, their behavior does not bear the same relationship to the consequences of their communication as ours bears to the consequences of our linguistic utterances.

There is yet another property of our language that distinguishes it from nonhuman forms of communication. That is its essential independence of the physical characteristics of the information transmitted. If we tape-record "give me your paw" and play it back to the puppy at the wrong speed, we get nothing from him even though the wrong speed provides frequencies well within the range of the dog's pitch sensitivity. The stimulus-response sequences governing the behavior of clouds and dogs are far more dependent upon quantitative aspects of the "input" than is language. It is this feature of language that underlies our notions of "meaning." We describe a stimulus as having "meaning" in the linguistic sense when its effects upon its recipient are essentially invariant over a wide range of physical transformations. We know the lyrics whether sung by soprano or bass. We comprehend a poem whether read or written. And, because of this dimension of meaning, we can even interpolate the proper elements missing in interrupted communication. We have all had the experience of a bad telephone connection in which the party on the other end comes through in "chopped" fashion. With difficulty, we follow. But what happens when the "mating call" of the bull elk is played back with fluttering interruptions? From research already conducted in this area, we can assume that the female doesn't understand a word he is saying. In short, we say a communication is *meaningful* when the effects it has upon the behavior of a recipient cannot be predicted solely from its physical characteristics. Put another way, while a physical medium is necessary, the medium is *not* the message. It is in this respect that language is meaningful and that we define language as *meaningful communication*. This sidesteps the issue of intention but does not dismiss it.

The last feature of language that distinguishes it from nonhuman forms of communication is not that it *can* be but that it *must* be taught. We impose this criterion to remove language from the domain of grunts and songs that fill a manless world. When we say that it must be taught, we are only acknowledging that language contains both sounds and rules that enable each member of the society to communicate with every other member. If he is not taught these sounds and rules, his communications will be *vocal* but not *linguistic;* he may be able to *signify* but not to *symbolize.* That is, he may employ gestures and sounds that mimic observable nature, but he will not be able to transmit symbolically information that describes the nonphysical aspects of nature, including his own nature. Because of this limitation, he will be able to communicate only with those in range of his physical existence. Communication limited to signs can inform posterity of things, but not thoughts. It will allow the depiction of the right triangle but not its theorem. It may permit a judgment of causes but not reasons.

## THE PROBLEM OF ACQUISITION

Languages are composed of sounds, technically called *phonemes.* All the words in the English language can be formed by combinations of some fifty phonemes. These words (strings of phonemes) are called *morphemes,* and the rules by which they are combined to create sentences are, collectively, the *grammar* of the language. We can write down the English-language phonemes on one piece of paper. With a not-too-thick dictionary, we can record all the morphemes in the English language. But there is no book thick enough for us to record all the grammatically correct sentences in English or any other language, because the number is infinite. With a relatively small set of grammatical rules, we are able to generate an infinite number of correct (although not necessarily meaningful) sentences. For example, there is nothing grammatically wrong with the sentence "The stool spent five chairs on the way to the sun." We can even impose meaning on it, if we are tolerant.

While infinity cannot be multiplied, language is still richer than what would be expected—even given the potential infinity of sentences. Culturally developed nuances, metaphors, dialects, and the like, collaborate with intonation, posture, gestures, and facial expressions to add further to the bounty of verbal communication. Granting this awesome variety, it seems almost incredible that nearly every educated adult can comprehend nearly every sentence expressed in his native tongue. How has this knowledge been gained? The controversy surrounding this question dates at least as far back as Leibniz's rejoinder to Locke's empiricism. Leibniz, the nativist, offered the now-traditional argument against the empiricist contention that all knowledge accrues from experience. If experience is to have any effect, Leibniz insisted, it must have its effect upon *something;* there must be an entity or a condition that preexists. Kant's *a priori* knowledge is based upon the same consideration. The nativist-empiricist tension finds fertile ground in theories of language. Emprically disposed theorists want language to be just one more behavior we learn at mother's knee. They attempt to apply to language the same associationistic principles that have, with varying success, explained other forms of "musculo-skeletal" learning. But language has not surrendered as easily as the bar press. To begin with, at mother's knee very little attention is given to grammar. Mother "reinforces" *what* the baby says, not how he says it. "Baby bye-bye" is more likely to be praised than is the more grammatical "Mommy is dopey." Then, too, children around the world begin to speak grammatically correct sentences at very nearly the same age, and it is doubtful that maternal instruction unfolds with such precise timing from Rangoon to Burbank. Children also come to follow the commands and lessons of adult speech long before they can create it themselves. In other words, while the comprehension of grammatical speech exists, the ability to create it does not; and this is not the kind of thing we confront in the usual operant conditioning setting. Children born to deaf mutes and reared in settings that preclude contact with verbal adults do not use language, although they can acquire it in remarkably rapid time. Similarly, when identical twins are reared under widely varying conditions of early motor training (one twin encouraged to crawl and later climb and run and jump; the other given no such inducement), the "impoverished" twin, when he has reached a certain level of maturity, catches up so quickly in basic motor abilities that one is hard-pressed to ascertain which one received which treatment. The similarity in studies of the acquisition of language among children reared by mutes has encouraged some to speculate that similar "innate" predispositions are responsible for linguistic behavior as those involved in walking or climbing.

The problem of "serial order" (discussed in Chapter 5) arises again in connection with language. The more mechanical varieties of associationist theory assume that chains of behavior develop because each response element serves as the stimulus for the next. Verbal behavior simply will not permit this. When we speak or read aloud, hundreds of muscle groups, consisting of tens of thousands of innervated muscle fibers, must engage in exquisitely coordinated patterns of responding. The interval between the expression of one sound and the one that immediately follows it is far too short for the sensory consequences of the first to serve as cues for the determination of the second. Instead, speech unfolds continuously and rhythmically, as if prepackaged and timed by some central organizing mechanism—a kind of language generator. The rhythms appear in every culture, as do the rules of grammar themselves. They appear at more or less fixed points in maturation. And they seem to have undergone no detectable change over the entire history of language. All these features combine to excite the notion of some kind of *innate* process. The analogy often used is that of a computer. Once certain design elements have been built in, the computer's response to inputs is determined. It can, for example, provide an infinite number of sums, but only because it is wired to *add*. Similarly (?), the adult can generate an infinite number of grammatically correct sentences, but only because he has been "wired" to connect morphemes in a determined way. The same process is invoked to account for the concert pianist in Chapter 5; once the piece has been thoroughly learned, the first eliciting stimulus calls forth an entire ensemble of responses. The chain unfolds *as a chain*. It is, to use a popular term, *preplanned* in that it will run its course, ignoring any input that happens to occur during its "readout." According to this view, we may teach—indeed we must teach—our children morphemes; but, beyond that, the built-in rules of grammar will permit the generation of sentences.

As with most nativistic arguments, precisely what has been "built in" or how it got built in is not entirely clear. Surely the genes don't know a noun from a participle. In fact, if the genes were the culprits, we would expect identical twins to be as similar in their creative expressions of language as they are in height and weight. Of course, these putative "innate rules" apply to the entire species; therefore, twins can be no more alike than any other two people for the simple reason that, with respect to these rules, we are *all* identical. But if this is so, then the great diversity of linguistic expression must finally be attributable to environmental differences. So we are right back at the start of the debate.

What the empiricist and the nativist do have in common is their emphasis upon the "in." Whether acquired or preplanned, our linguistic abilities are presumed to be "in" the brain. It shouldn't be at all surprising that any science that can offer us an "emotion center" without a trace of embarrassment will have little trouble giving us one for language.

## LANGUAGE AND THE BRAIN

In 1861, the French physician Pierre-Paul Broca reported the results of an autopsy performed on a patient who suffered from, among other maladies, *aphasia* (the inability to speak with any coherence). Broca found a lesion in the cerebral cortex—specifically, in the posterior portion of the frontal lobe just above the lip of the temporal cortex (see Figure 8-1). Now known as "Broca's area" it quickly passed into the literature as the "speech center." It is on the *dominant* side of the cortex, the left side in right-handed individuals and even in many individuals judged to be left-handed.

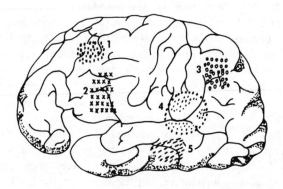

**FIGURE 8-1**

Cortical areas associated with symbolic communication. Sketch of human (left) cortical hemisphere indicating the areas which, when diseased or injured, give rise to communications disorders. (1) writing disturbances (agraphia, dysgraphia); (2) *Broca's area* (expressive and/or receptive aphasias); (3) reading disturbances (alexia, dyslexia); (4) Wernicke's area, associated with "word deafness"; (5) naming disturbances (agnosias).

As evidence mounted, it became clear that no one specific region of the cerebral cortex is exclusively responsible for language. Figure 8-1 shows the relatively broad distribution of cortical regions associated with language pathology (when diseased) and language disturbances (when electrically stimulated). Language disturbances take a multitude of forms, but all can be classified as either (a) receptive, (b) expressive, or (c) mixed. The receptive disturbances may involve the inability to recognize written words or symbols (alexia), spoken words (aphasia), or melodies (amelodia). The expressive forms include the inability to speak (motor aphasia), to perform simple arithmetic operations (acalculia), to write (agraphia), or to pronounce words articulately (dysarthria). Typically, these conditions result from vascular lesions (blood clots, ruptured vessels, etc.) and tumors. Interestingly, many patients who have undergone lobotomies for psychiatric disturbances, and who may have had some surgical destruction of "Broca's area," have not subsequently displayed language pathology. Also, massive surgery involving the removal of an entire (malignant) hemisphere does not remove linguistic ability—even when it is the dominant hemisphere that has been removed—*if the patient is a very young child.* That is, if the language abilities have not already become localized, the nondominant hemisphere can come to serve these linguistic functions.[2]

The disproportionate representation of language skills on the left side has led to intriguing findings obtained from human patients who have undergone a corpus callosectomy. The corpus callosum is the dense band of fibers connecting the two hemispheres. In certain forms of epilepsy, seizures of an electrical nature begin on one side of the brain and then develop in the corresponding location on the other side. If the second "focus" does not develop, generalized seizures will not occur. To prevent the development of the second and crucial focus, the two hemispheres are surgically disconnected. Surprisingly, patients who have endured callosal sectioning appear "normal" in virtually every respect despite the severing of the most massive association tract in the brain. On closer examination, however, we find interesting consequences of surgery. If the patient is given an object in his left hand (whose sensory information is delivered to the right hemisphere) he is completely unable to name it. When placed in the right hand, which projects to the left (dominant) hemisphere, it is recognized immediately. What seems to be happening is this: Information delivered to the left hand is transmitted to a region of cortex devoid of linguistic elements. Thus, the object can be felt, but it cannot be named.[3]

This is the kind of finding that could prompt one to exclaim, "Aha; language is on the left side!" But what could such a statement possibly mean? From stimulation studies of monkey and man, we know that certain areas lead to *vocalization.* The lips move, the tongue taps the roof of the mouth, the diaphragm forces air across the vocal cords, and sounds are thereby generated. This is obviously not evidence for a "language center"—any more than getting the fingers dancing is evidence for a "concerto" center. Again we face the two-headed villain: reason and cause. Brain activity is the cause of speech to the same extent that it is the cause of walking. Broca knew that a century ago; Galen, tens of centuries earlier. But this fact does *nothing* to elucidate the physiological basis of *language*. Most discouraging of all, we cannot even safely conclude that the problem is a technical one. Let us assume, for the sake of charity, that we get even smaller electrodes, less noisy amplifiers, more willing patients, better means of stimulation, recording, and data analysis. With this embellished armamentarium, we strike out eagerly and find that when a certain collection of cells is stimulated, only adverbs are produced! Best of all, when we record from these cells in conscious man, they "fire" every time he utters an adverb. Taking fancy a step further, we find that these cells produce a unique substance which, when injected into a duck, finds the duck quacking adverbs! And, finally, children reared on a diet of such ducks come to acquire the adverbial form more quickly than "control" children reared on "naïve" ducks. With this information, or any equivalent form of it, what would

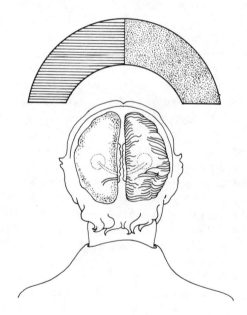

**FIGURE 8-2**
Split-brain man. The sketch shows the severed corpus callosum and the projection of visual material to each side separately. (Adapted from Michael S. Gazzaniga, *The Bisected Brain*. New York: Appleton-Century-Crofts. Copyright © 1970 by Meredith Corporation. Reprinted by permission of Appleton-Century-Crofts, Educational Division, Meredith Corporation.)

we be prepared to say about the biological basis of language? How do mental abstractions become chemical codes? How does the cell come to respond to the meaning? These questions are not raised to be argumentative. It is simply essential to acknowledge that we do not escape the difficulties of explaining complex psychological functions by attributing them to cells rather than to man. Taking a noun out of the mind and putting it into a neuron leaves the fundamental question intact. We still have to determine the basis upon which the neuron treats it as a noun.

Even the patient with a sectioned callosum (see Figure 8–2), in so many respects a windfall to those engaged in research on the neural basis of speech, has raised at least as many questions as he has been able to answer. When we show an object to his right hemisphere (by presenting it to the temporal retina of his right eye), he cannot tell us what it is. We ask, "Do you know what was flashed?" and he may report that he has seen nothing. We now present the same stimulus (e.g., the letter *W*) to the temporal retina of the left eye, and he unhesitatingly announces "W." But can we be confident that his failure on the earlier trial was due to a *linguistic* deficit? To what extent is his inability to articulate the sound a reliable indicator of his not "knowing" what the stimulus is? In short, what are the cues by which we come to "know" anything? When do we know that we know?

## THE RETREAT TO EMERGENTISM

When two atoms of hydrogen are combined with one of sulfur and four of oxygen, we get something that is unlike either hydrogen or sulfur or oxygen. We get sulfuric acid. Sooner or later, those who have speculated at length on the relationship between brain activity and mind activity have adopted the notion of *emergent* properties— properties that are not simply reducible to the added influences of their constituents. In psychology, it was the Gestalt psychologists, rejecting the reductionism of the empiricists, who emphasized the emergent properties of perception. A triangle, for example, is perceptually more than and different from three lines; it has a form, a cohesiveness, a "truth" that cannot be deduced from a knowledge of straight lines. Consciousness, that gray figure who has haunted la Mettrie's machine for two centuries, would seem to be a condition that emerges from the neural mix of which our brains are made. It appears to be more a fact than a thing. In this respect, it is not unique in nature. Gravity, relativity, time—these are facts. They are conditions of nature that transform matter without being matter. Few have said it as well as the American poet Richard Wilbur:

Mind in its purest play is like some bat
That beats about in caverns all alone.
Contriving by a kind of senseless wit
Not to conclude against a wall of stone.

It has no need to falter or explore;
Darkly it knows what obstacles are there,
And so may weave and flitter, dip and soar
In perfect courses through the blackest air.

And has this simile a like perfection?
The mind is like a bat. Precisely. Save
That in the very happiest intellection
A graceful error may correct the cave.[4]

The consciousness that authored such lines is not "in" Broca's area. Damage to "speech centers" may well preclude such songs, but this no more places the songs in the centers than would the effects of a laryngectomy place them in the throat.

Accepting consciousness in these terms does not imply a metaphysical view, less a spiritual one. For all we know, everything in the universe is "conscious" just as all things, including ourselves, may consider themselves "human." What distinguishes us from the rest is not necessarily what we are but what we *say* we are. And, when we listen to Shakespeare, or Voltaire, or Dante, when we observe the canvasses of Leonardo, or are moved by Beethoven, we begin to realize that whatever it is we've been saying all these centuries, *it* is surely not "on the left side."

## UNIVERSALS AND THE POSSIBLE LIMITS OF UNDERSTANDING

So, are Socrates standing and Socrates seated the same? And what is horse and what is mind? There are facts that have been bared by our studies of neurophysiology that may be portentous. Let's look again at the "bug" detectors of the frog and the cortical cells in the visual system of the cat. The frog fixes himself in the weeded pond, a creature with perhaps but one idea. The arrangement of neural elements in his retina is such that, no matter what the real world is or does, the only "truth" is that black convexity moving across his eye. With the suddenness of a mathematical insight, his sensory-motor linkage solves the problem, activates the muscles of the tongue, and removes one more fly from the land of the living.[5] We cannot ask the frog whether a standing and a seated Socrates are the same, but we can ask whether a stationary and a moving fly are. To the frog, they are not. It is in the limitations of his nervous system that the *universal,* the Platonically "true" fly must move. As we ascend the phylogenetic ladder, the Universals become more fluid. The cortical cells of the cat can accommodate both the fly that moves and the one that doesn't. Different sets of units are tied to each of these stimulus properties. Neurally, the cat *can* know (whether he actually does or not) that FLY embraces a far broader genre than the frog could ever expect. The fly, himself, treats cats and frogs and nearly anything else that moves in much the same way; we call him "fly" for a reason. We may speculate that this poor creature knows only two states of reality, the moving and the still. He can be destroyed by almost anything with momentum and is equipped with sensory-motor mechanisms lacking the luxury of subtle distinctions. To be sure, his sensors are keen and, by themselves, may respond with extraordinary precision to small changes in the environment. But the fly *as fly* either eats or runs. All the information being processed elegantly by his receptors finally becomes translated into one of two instructions. And what of us? We share much with cats and even frogs and flies. What are our Universals? Are there "truths" all around that our neurons cannot process? Are the truths we've found more an expression of the peculiarities of our neurophysiology than a reflection of the way the world behaves? We, too, have exquisite sensory equipment, capable of responding differentially to the very subtlest of events. But does all this detail ultimately get flattened and diluted by stereotyped decision mechanisms?

We generally think of consciousness as an "awareness of self." Nature seems to have something akin to this; we call it evolution, and we witness it in every sphere of organization from the zygote that becomes a man to the tribe that reaches the age of Pericles. We often lose sight of the fact that the brains we carry in our current heads are not the last word in nervous systems. We also find it convenient to ignore the individual evolution—the *ontogenesis*—of brain function that results from cultivation. Enrichment changes the brain, and isolation kills it. We have it on the very best authorities—the fools and giants of history—that a few good ideas are often more than enough to rescue an entire nation and that a few bad ones can wreck it in a decade. Often, in our impatience with the problems of existence, we take these elementary facts and try to convince ourselves that, if we just accelerate evolution a bit, paradise is ours. Today this innocence finds expression in utopias fashioned by "conditioning" or, better, by brain surgery. We can, after all, make cats and mice and even men placid with electrodes. We can turn "aggression" on and off. We can alter eating habits, maternal behavior, sexuality, dreams. We can "perfect" man or at least greatly improve his lot with any one of several methods: conditioning, psychosurgery, genetic engineering. The problem, of course, is that we haven't been able to fathom just what this man should be. Accelerating evolution is not so difficult, since it is largely a technical problem. Far more perplexing is *anticipating* it, and that is a philosophical problem, but one that only future philosophers will be able to solve. By then, of course, the transition will be effected and philosophers will have to be again content with reporting rather than ordaining.

Presumably, future man will bear a fair resemblance to ourselves. His differences will evolve from our similarities. To these similarities, volumes have been devoted. A recurrent theme—expressed by Aristotle, by Leibniz, by Kant, and, in modern times, by Piaget, Freud, and Lorenz—is one that grants us certain inborn dispositions. Aristotle and Kant attempted to reduce these dispositions to an irreducible set of *categories*. In Kant's epistemology, all human knowledge finally reduces to the categories of *quantity, quality, relation,* and *modality*. From the category of quantity emerge the concepts of one, many, and all (i.e., singularity, plurality, totality). From quality arise *reality, negation,* and *limitation* (e.g., that a premise or event is so, or is not so, or is so within limits). Relation spawns the concepts of *causality* and that of *community* (in modern terms, *correlation*) and that of *substance,* by which we appreciate the unchanging nature of things. Under the category *modality* rest the concepts of *possibility, existence,* and *necessity* (i.e., that $X$ could be, that $X$ is, that $X$ must be). For Kant, these are the "pure concepts," present in us *a priori.* Were they not, experience would be meaningless. In other words, Kant dismissed the empiricist contention that the human understanding is formed by experience alone. Clearly, if *a priori* capacities (categories, concepts, biases, etc.) did not exist, the torrents of environmental stimuli could never become organized.

Kant was not a physiologist, and his writings are not explicitly "scientific." Yet, buried in his *Categories* is the germ of a neurological theory. If the mind is prearranged to organize the elements of experience, there is at least presumptive evidence for corresponding brain mechanisms possessing analogous properties. We can employ the concept of *causality* illustratively. We tend to think of $A$ as causing $B$ when we observe that $B$ always follows $A$ and that $A$ always precedes $B$. In other words, the *evidence* for causation is empirical, while, in Kantian terms, the *concept* of causation is categorical and *a priori.* That is, if the concept did not exist, the experiences would not enjoy their subjective reliability. Neurally, there is a temporal limit imposed upon our ability to detect sequences. Sensory fibers can respond only so quickly and no more. For example, if two lights are flashed sequentially, with the termination of the first occurring 1 msec earlier than the commencement of the second, we will see only one flash. The two will be completely fused. If we call the first *A* and the second *B,* and if, in fact, the onset of *A* is an event that causes *B,* we will have no sense of causation. Since the events occur at a rate too rapid for our discriminative capacities, we will insist that only one event occurred. In other words, we find in the limitations of our nervous system the possible limitation of our ability to recognize causal dependencies. In any sequence of (in fact) causally dependent events *a, b, c, . . . j,* we will "understand" that *a* causes *j* directly if the intervals between *a* and *b, b* and *c, . . . i* and *j* are too short for temporal resolution.

The foregoing involves but the simplest of discriminations. In complex judgmental settings, we also require the mediation of neural processes and these are limited. They are limited not only in the sense of quantitative functions but also qualitatively. When Kant speaks of *possibility, existence,* and *necessity,* he might unwittingly be describing fixed operating characteristics of our nervous systems. We conceive of possibilities by induction; of existence, by demonstration; of necessity, by deduction. We call the first a *hypothesis,* the second a *fact,* and the third a *law.* Hypotheses are inextricably bound to perception and memory. Facts are immediately appealing to the senses. Laws are—what? By virtue of what process do we conclude not that a relationship exists but that it *must* exist; that its contrary alternative is *impossible;* that it is *logically necessary?* I submit that the basis for such laws is not essentially different from the basis upon which, for the frog, a dark, moving convexity *must be* a fly. If we grant imagination to the frog, we can ascertain the type of "law" this amphibian might discover. We arrange an image of a bird from whose beak dark convexities emerge. When the frog croaks, an "optical fly" is released. The resulting "law"—ASK AND YOU SHALL RECEIVE—is as predictable as it is preposterous. The important point here is not that the frog can be conditioned or even that he can be fooled. The important point is that he *must* be conditioned and he *must,* per force, be fooled. That is, given his neural nuances, the correlation between croaking and flies must come to be conceived as a law just as the moving spot must be seen as a fly. [6]

The familiar "cave allegory" in the *Republic* was offered by Plato as evidence against the senses. The cave dwellers, chained before a parapet, are victims of illusion. Relying on their senses, they fail to recognize the true causes responsible for the events occurring before them. One of them escapes, ascends into the light, learns the truth, and returns to free his comrades. Predictably, he is chided for being blinded by the light of day. But what Plato failed to acknowledge is that the deceptions of the senses are not evaded by an exercise of nonsensory reason. The senses deceive because of the inherent limitations imposed by structure and functional physiology; for instance, human vision is unresponsive to wavelengths longer than 780–800 nanometers. But the brain has its own peculiarities; for instance, we fail to "see" the first of two stimuli if the second is more intense and follows the first even with a delay as great as 200 msec. In such a setting, our "reason" can be based only upon the properties of the more intense stimulus, since the weaker one is not represented in the system at all. Thus, Plato's cave dweller may have discovered that his senses betrayed his wits but was not aware of the possibility of his wits betraying his wits. When the scientist J. B. S. Haldane suggests that nature is not only queerer than we suspect but queerer than *we can* suspect, he is recognizing that the functional limitations of our neural processes may permanently decide the manner in which we will "know" reality.

## STATES VS. MECHANISMS

I've alluded often to the difference between a "state" or "condition" of activity and a mechanism. When we say that the brain is a new system, we are proposing that the same structures—indeed, the same basic mechanisms—are constantly in the process of *becoming;* that the principal attribute of neural tissue is *potentiality.* We can witness this property in many contexts. The effect of prismatic distortion in visual perception is illustrative. If a subject is equipped with optical prisms, the world becomes instantly reversed, and coordinated behavior is impossible. Left is right, right is left, and utter confusion reigns. However, after several hours, performance improves. In several days, it is very nearly perfect. The great Kepler, in the seventeenth century, showed that the retinal image of the world is inverted, and all enlightened men knew that the brain converted this to a right-side-up condition. *But how?* And how does the modern experimental subject come to reverse the sensory-motor habits of a lifetime in just several days? We shouldn't expect to comprehend the means by which this is achieved through a study of mechanisms (cell metabolism, single-unit recordings, etc.). Clearly, what is involved is a change in the *state*—the functional organization—of massive numbers of units. When our subject says to himself, "Aha! Right is now left and left is right," there is a correlated shift in the manner in which the nervous system, *en masse,* proceeds to process information and initiate behavior. By analogy, it is as if the system had an "invert" control, much as a tape recorder can be reversed. The basic mechanisms of tape recording are not affected when we reverse the direction of the spools. In fact, we can conceive of a nervous system that could understand only the reversed message and that, at the same time, consisted of the same units and mechanisms as our own. We might even argue that the subject who has adapted to prismatic distortion possesses such a system. As we descend the phylogenetic series, this type of adaptation quickly becomes a rarity and soon an impossibility. The infant newt, for example, can have his eyes twisted through 180 degrees, replaced in their orbits, and grow to maturity. No matter how long the adult lives with this reversal of reality, he still juts his tongue to the left when a fly is placed to the right. Whatever the human subject's system is doing during the period of adaptation, the newt's can't. Yet, the mechanisms of impulse initiation, synaptic transmission, unit discharges, etc., probably are not very different in the two. In these two systems, then, every particular process is probably the same while every general property is different. This is what the Gestaltists are getting at with a term such as "emergentism." It is to the individual nervous system what evolution is to the species. This is why it may be futile to examine "output" properties in an attempt to comprehend the functional states of the systems that generate them. The failure of reductionism is thus wed to its success. If it were correct in treating complex systems as but the sum of simple ones, and we know that simple ones are devoid of psychological character, then—

## AND NOW

Let us now try to develop certain guidelines whenever and if ever we use the words "mind" and "brain" interchangeably. The first is that any such statement be restricted to a specification of *causes,* not *reasons.* The position taken here is that *causes* involve mechanisms and that reasons may or may not. At present, we must conclude that intentionality has not been reduced to mechanistic description. Moreover, it is not clear that this failure is traceable to technical limitations. That is, the language used to describe intentionality (i.e., *reasons*) so differs from that adequate to specify causes that a version of parallelism seems unavoidable. Causes can be described topographically, kinetically, energetically. We can speak of the latencies and amplitudes of efferent impulses, the area of motor cortex that is active, the number of muscle fibers activated. Reasons are described evaluatively, affectively, and phenomenally. We can speak of recognizing an act as "proper," "pleasing," and "inescapable." But propriety, pleasure, and dilemma are not isomorphic with latency, amplitude, number, and the like. Stimulation of posterior hypothalamus in man may lead to the statement "I want to kill you." If such is the case, we may legitimately speak of hypothalamic activation as the cause of the utterance but not the reason for the feeling. Indeed, we may say that the *reason* derives from the individual's ability to reflect upon the feeling and to assign a value to it. The reflective capacity (consciousness, or Kant's *apperception*) is the *a priori* condition or state without which the hypothalamic event could not result in the utterance. To discover that, in every instance of homicide, the murderous act reliably followed a spate of hypothalamic activity would only be to learn *how* homicide occurs and not *why*. The former is addressed to causes and can, therefore, be described in terms of mechanisms. The latter refers to reasons and is explicable only in terms that may not reduce to physiological processes.

One may ask whether this implies that our reasons are uncaused. That is, are we suggesting that our reasons are the uncaused, spontaneous causes of neural events, which, in turn, cause action? The answer is a decisive *no*. Instead, the suggestion is that psychological reasons bear the same relationship to neural causes that a blueprint bears to a house. There is nothing in the blueprint that will tell us where the house is to be built, of what it is to be made, who will occupy it, how it will be affected by the seasons. Subsequently, we can look at the completed structure and, from its dimensions, reconstruct the drawings upon which it was based. Yet no amount of knowledge of its tiles, bricks, plumbing fixtures, etc., will be of the least assistance in redrawing the blueprints. Thus, in one sense, the house *is* bricks, gutters, steps, etc. In another, different, and equally valid sense, the house *is* the blueprint. The physical elements are what cause the house to be. The blueprint is the *rational* and *a priori* consideration without which the house cannot exist. In spite of this architectural metaphor, reasons are not to be considered the emergent products of *structure*. Anatomical arrangements, per se, cannot tell us why certain of them are chosen and not others in a given situation. Thus, the architecture of the nervous system limits *how* we might reason but cannot be said to cause *that* we reason. This fact leads to parallelism; to an acceptance of a qualitative difference between mental and physical events; to the inability to specify the former in terms of the latter; to a view of mental and neural activity as abiding correlates, with the former being the cause of reasons and the latter the cause of actions.

With respect to actions, we must understand how the term "cause" is used. By *causes*, we mean only that certain measurable events of a neural nature always precede certain measurable events of a behavioral nature and that elimination of the former is sufficient to preclude the appearance of the latter. Satisfying this criterion is no defence against coincidence.

Another guideline is this: The methods of science are not yet able to accommodate private experiences nor are they likely to. This is simply another way of stating that knowledge is not readily translated from one level of explanation to another; that scientific demonstration occurs in a context that is not unfailingly generalizable to unregulated domains. Wittingly or otherwise, the neural sciences have been far more effective in creating the impression of success with psychological matters than they have been in fact. They have been too quick to perceive an advance in neuro*physiology ipso facto,* as a development in neuro*psychology.* Our reliance upon data gathered from studies of lower animals has recreated the problem of anthropomorphism to an extent that would astound even pre-Darwinians. We have been all too comfortable in treating the mechanical *reactions* of subhumans as if they were prototypic of the dynamic *actions* of man. We have understated the very substantial discrepancies found when human patients have been exposed to treatments comparable to those employed in studies of subhumans.

Opposing the foregoing, I have attempted to present the many considerable achievements in neuropsychology; the evolution of a more precise and useful understanding of functional relationships between brain activity and behavior. Questions are now phrased with greater care. Multiple techniques abound where, earlier, only one might serve to support an ambitious generalization. More and more, leaders in the field show a respect for the vitality of those issues that just a decade ago were not mentioned in polite neuropsychological circles. We no longer dismiss the philosophical turmoil of the eighteenth and nineteenth centuries as futile. We now wonder aloud about the problems of identity and isomorphism; whether brain events and mental events are but two manifestations of the same phenomenon as, for example, matter and energy. We admit also the relevance of distinctions between contingency and necessity. There is overwhelming evidence supporting the assertion that specifiable conditions *do* obtain in the nervous system when psychological events occur. Whether they *must* and, if so, which ones must are different questions. There is even a serious revival of mentalism, which, while not especially helpful, nurtures a condition of wholesome skepticism that never exists in its absence. We can now discover, even in the experimental journals, reasoned speculation on the possibility of mental events being nonphysical—more precisely, mental events being of a nature that precludes complete physical specification. We have yet to revive the more haunting variety of dualism that finds the brain obeying the dictates of the mind; but, with more and more interest in yoga and in Eastern thought in general, we may even have a go with that one again. There are cycles to these things; from matter as mind, to mind as matter, to mind over matter, to mind doesn't matter. The healthiest cycle is the uncertain one, and I hope it isn't too optimistic to think we've entered it. Nearly everyone in the neural sciences is coming to recognize that yawning breach between the thick catalog of facts and the thin "Book of Truth." Most important, this recognition has not led to dour pessimism. Leaving the mind aside, the brain is fascinating in its own right, and I hope that I've conveyed some of its allure in these few pages. It is not a small thing to anchor behavioral and perceptual processes to neural mechanisms. In fact, had the aspirations of the nineteenth century been more realistic, recent achievements could be a source of unbridled enthusiasm. But the nineteenth century was not content merely to escape the challenges of philosophy. It had to insist as well that the challenges were artificial and that the methods of science would show them to be trivial. "Localization of function" became the rallying cry of those who would presume to treat moral and ethical matters of *value* as if they were merely questions of *fact*. The clinic and the laboratory did much to make the slogan a principle, and even the monumental efforts of Lashley could not completely diminish the conviction. Indeed, his efforts tended to foster the view that the problem really was experimental rather than conceptual. While he successfully illustrated that learning and memory are not "here" or "there," he still left room for the question of "where" "they" were. For many years, the ethologists—who have always been puzzled by the way psychologists describe and study animal behavior—were virtually excluded from participation. This, too, has been reversed. We know now that when we use the word "learning," we mean more than left turns in a runway and bar-presses for food. We recognize that such words refer to *states* of activity in a system *as a whole*.[7] Modern computers assist this maturing perspective by allowing us to extract some meaning statistically from that cauldron of neuroelectric furor we call the brain. And, we are coming to appreciate the highly statistical flavor of brain activity. Where the nineteenth century bequeathed a mechanical monolith, we offer our heirs a more time-varying, flexible, and probabilistic system, which, in these terms, can be treated and described as a whole. La Mettrie's englightened machine—like Condillac's "sentient statue," who derived all knowledge by passively awaiting the good works of the environment—is no more. We recognize the intrinsic life of the brain: its self-pacing, self-scanning rhythms; its functional malleability; its spatial shifts in peak activity; its duty/rest cycles. It is in this century that we've produced a brain that has any chance of hosting a mind. But because of these huge gains, we're plagued by the impatience of rising expectations, and we lapse into those very styles of thinking that we ourselves showed to be outmoded. The lapses take several forms: conveniently repressing the reality of problems of definition; smoothly gliding past an issue of experimental control; facilely assuming the comparability of conditions that in fact have little in common; worst of all, believing our supporters more than our critics. Nevertheless,these are lapses and not abiding conditions. The nineteenth century arrived at and remained in this state out of unshakable conviction. We slip back out of momentary fatigue, and we don't remain long. Of course, the nineteenth century let us happen, and our debt must be greater than our derision. Even at their physicalistic best, they left room for a romantic moment. It was in that century that one prominent scientist described every living thing as "a melody that sings itself." Neuropsychology is learning how to listen.

## NOTES AND REFERENCES

1. A concise review of theories of language is provided by R. Terwilliger, *Meaning And Mind: A Study In The Psychology Of Language* (New York: Oxford Univ. Press, 1968).
2. Still the most interesting treatise on relations between brain mechanisms and language is that of W. Penfield & L. Roberts, *Speech And Brain Mechanisms* (Princeton, N.J.: Princeton Univ. Press, 1959).
3. A thorough review of the still skimpy literature on "split-brain man" has been provided by M. S. Gazzaniga, *The Bisected Brain* (New York: Appleton-Century, 1970).
4. From *Things of This World,* © 1956, by Richard Wilbur. Reprinted by permission of Harcourt Brace Jovanovich, Inc. Also reprinted by permission of Faber and Faber Ltd. from *Poems 1943–1956.*
5. A "must" reading is J. Y. Lettvin, H. Maturana, W. McCulloch & W. Pitts, "What the Frog's Eye Tells The Frog's Brain," *Proc. I.R.E.,* 1959, *47,* 1940–1951.
6. Kant, as it happens, did toy with the idea that his "categories" might be explained in biological terms but rejected the possibility on the grounds that such determination would render the categories merely *contingent* rather than *necessary.*

7. See, especially, Karl Pribram's *Languages Of The Brain* (Englewood Cliffs, N.J.: Prentice-Hall, 1971).

# Index of Names

155

# Subject Index